POLITICS & LETTERS

NCQ TITLES

Legal Fictions
Politics & Letters
On Yeats: Upon a House
Drama & Democracy
Locating Theology
Time Pieces
Critical Paranoia
On Joyce: 3 easy essays
On Eliot
Literary Conversions

Film texts

A Trip to Rome
A Short Break in Budapest
Magic in Prague
A Week in Venice
Four Days in Athens
The Last Priest of Horus
WWW: the weekend that warped the world

Play texts

Darwin: an evolutionary entertainment
Strange Meetings & Shorts

Eliotics

In preparation

Rubbishing Hockney & other reviews
On Collecting Walter Benjamin
Autobiography & Class Consciousness
Considering Canterbury Cathedral

Though each can be read independently, these NCQ publications, taken together, comprise a single hyper-text collection.

POLITICS & LETTERS

SELECTED ESSAYS

Bernard Sharratt

New Crisis Quarterly
2015

NEW CRISIS QUARTERLY

ncq@newcrisisquarterly.myzen.co.uk

First published 2015

ISBN : 978-1-910956-00-7

In memory of
Raymond Williams
with gratitude

CONTENTS

FOREWORD

This short book brings together a number of essays, arranged in more or less historical order, from the 15th century to nearly the present, which explore various aspects of the relations between an author or a body of writing and politics. Together they indicate a range of critical methods and concerns.

The pieces appeared in various periodicals and collections, some dating back to the 1970s. Various shifts in political and intellectual concerns since those decades might well be traced in these various contributions. That they remain discrete essays perhaps indicates sufficiently the continuing difficulty of arriving at any satisfactory overall methodological, theoretical, or even political position within what used to be known as 'literary criticism'. Given the current near-obsolescence of that very term, I am happy to record the personal influence of two mentors, F. R. Leavis and Raymond Williams, alongside the continuing impact of an ever-productive contemporary, and old friend, Terry Eagleton.

The essays do not pay much direct attention to some more recent preoccupations among literary scholars and cultural critics, including my own. From the 1980s I was more preoccupied with the implications of computer technologies than with literary theory and its successors. It is indeed one of those digital developments, the rise of do-it-yourself print-on-demand publishing that has prompted me to publish this book, and some other accompanying titles which are more concerned with later issues.

Publishing essays is at best a minor contribution. I once coined the phrase 'the Mrs. Gaskell syndrome' to indicate a familiar dilemma: when wondering what sort of political contribution it is possible to make to an issue, the writer often ends up writing about that issue in the hope of persuading readers to make up their minds about what contribution to make….

At least, putting together this small volume has thankfully taken up little of my time and few trees will have been sacrificed for it. Whether readers will waste their time in reading them, I really don't know. But at least self-publishing them will save my children from the familiar dilemma of wondering what to salvage from a study full of tattered typescripts and a computer full of old files.

The title of the collection pays homage to a periodical from the 1940s edited by Raymond Williams, entitled *Politics & Letters*, and it seemed appropriate to end this collection with a review of the volume of interviews with Williams also published under that title. My own tongue-in-cheek imprint, *New Crisis Quarterly*, revives another title, that of an exceedingly short-lived periodical: its first, only, and farewell issue appeared in 1984, under the guise of my *The Literary Labyrinth*. Its editorial programme was to publish reviews of books I didn't feel I had the time actually to write. Both the variously named reviewers and the variously authored reviewed books in *Literary Labyrinth* were therefore wholly imagined *personae*, but readers were invited, if so inclined, to write the books themselves.

Other *NCQ* books are rather more in the spirit of that editorial approach than this one, which is almost a proper book, but it too remains obviously incomplete, since there are, of course, many other writers and issues not considerd, though there are also overlaps with other *NCQ* titles, particularly perhaps *Drama and Democracy*, *Legal Fictions*, *Critical Paranoia*, and those on Yeats and Joyce.

However, the overall invitation to readers remains the same: to complete the work if they so wish—in this case the partly failed and partly defeated attempts of my generation of literary critics to make the consideration of relations between literature and politics a useful and effective contribution. I would now, if I had the time or the scholarship, re-write or correct some of these essays, but the underlying problems remain and in the present context some of those previous emphases are still, I think, worth recalling.

B.S.
1st May 2015

Acknowledgements

I am grateful to the publishers concerned for their permission to reprint some of these pieces, which originally appeared as follows:

Skelton, in *Medieval Literature : Literature, Criticism, Ideology*, edited by David Aers, Harvester Press, 1986.

Milton, in *Essays & Studies 1982*, edited by S. Bushrui, 1982, John Murray for the English Association.

Coleridge, in *New Blackfriars*, April & May 1970.

Morris, in *The Victorian Novel: detail into form*, edited by Ian Gregor, Vision Press, 1980.

Tressell, in *The Robert Tressell Lectures 1981-88*, edited by David Alfred, WEA, 1988.

'Writing Britains', in *British Cultural Studies: Geography, Nationality, and Identity* edited by David Morley & Kevin Robins, Oxford University Press, 2001. By permission of Oxford University Press.

'Inside the impasse', *Red Letters*, Summer 1980

*

JOHN SKELTON: FINDING A VOICE —
Notes after Bakhtin

Alexander Pope in 1737 glossed 'Skelton' thus: 'Poet Laureate to Hen. 8. a Volume of whose Verses has been lately reprinted, consisting almost wholly of Ribaldry, Obscenity, and Billingsgate Language'.[1] If, in a changed cultural climate, Pope's acid summary might actually induce curious readers to sample the recent Penguin edition of *The Complete English Poems* [2] of John Skelton, they might indeed alight upon some Billingsgate language:

> Now Gamyche, garde thy gummys;
> My serpentins and my gunnys
> Agenst ye now I bynde;
> Thy selfe therfore defende.
> Thou tode, thow scorpyon,
> Thow bawdy babyone,
> Thow bere, thow brystlyd bore,
> Thou Moryshe mantycore,
> Thou rammysche, stynkyng gote
> Thou fowle, chorlyshe parote,
> Thou gresly gargone glaymy ...
> (*Agenst Gamesche*, p. 128)

But readers are just as likely to encounter, say:

> *Moderata juvant* but toto dothe exede;
> Dyscrecion ys modyr of nobyll vertues all;
> *Myden agan* in Grekys tonge we rede,
> But reason and wytte wantythe theyr provynciall,

[1] In a note to Pope's 'Imitations of Horace', included in Edwards (1981), p. 75.

[2] Edited by John Scattergood (1983). Page references are to this edition, and I have generally checked my quotations against Scattergood's text, except for my own translations from Latin. The first modern edition was that of Alexander Dyce in 1843. There are now various facsimile editions, and a modernised version of the poems was published by Philip Henderson (revised, 1948).

When wylfulnes ys vicar generall
'*Hec res acu tangitur*, Parrott, *par ma foye*—'
'*Tycez-vous*, Parrott, *tenes-vous coye*.'
(*Speke Parott*, p. 232)

A preliminary flip through the substantial volume will reveal 150 pages of densely elucidatory notes, 50 pages of 'Select Glossary ', and—even more off-putting—the regular inclusion of French, Latin and Greek passages within the 'English ' poems themselves. Since, moreover, Skelton falls into a peculiar critical abyss—a poet of uncertain status awkwardly straddling convenient periodisations—the initial problem, it might seem, is not to encourage any fashionable *re*-reading of Skelton but simply to get him read at all

Yet it may be that the initial deterrent effect of multilingualism itself suggests a framework within which we can approach this unfamiliar writer, finding in his work a considerable overlap with some contemporary critical concerns.

Languages in Crisis

In the mid-thirteenth century Roger Bacon assumed that an educated Englishman should speak English, French and Latin '*sicut maternum in qua natus est* '. Two centuries later, the proto-Puritan, William Turner, sourly complained that some contemporary writers 'writ so french Englishe and so latine that no man except he be both a latin man, a french man and also an englishe man shalbe able to vnderstande their writinge'.[3]

Whereas in the fourteenth century Gower's three major works are each written in a different language (*Confessio Amantis* in English; *Vox Clamantis* in Latin; *Speculum Meditantis* in French), by the late sixteenth century "English' had been consolidated as the obvious medium of English poets, however extensively later poets were still to write also

---

[3] Cf. Roger Bacon, *Compendium studii philosophiae*, quoted in Salter (1983), pp. 26, 186, and William Turner, *The Sum of Divinitie* (1548), quoted in Jones (1953), p. 99.

in Latin (Donne, Jonson, Marvell, Milton). Yet 'English' long remains a problematic term: in 1490, England's first printer, William Caxton, in his Preface to his own translation of a French translation of the *Aeneid*, noted not only that 'comyn englysshe that is spoken in one shyre varyeth from another', but that in seeking 'to vse olde and homely termes' in his translations, the 'englysshe' in the 'olde bokes' he consulted was 'so rude and brood that I coude not wele vnderstande it', 'it was more lyke to dutche than englysshe' (Aurner, 1965, pp. 286-7).

In that same Preface by Caxton we find the first public mention of Skelton:

> But I praye mayster John Skelton late created poete laureate in the vnyuersite of oxenforde to ouersee and correcte this sayd booke . . For hym I knowe for suffycyent to expowne and englysshe euery dyffyculte that is therin/ For he hath late translated the epystlys of Tulle/ and the boke of dyodorus syculus. and diuerse other werkes oute of latyn in to englysshe not in rude and olde langage. but in polysshed and ornate termes craftely.

Skelton's translation of Cicero's *Familiar Letters* is lost, and his version of Diodorus Siculus (not directly from Greek but from the Italian Poggio's Latin translation) remained in manuscript until 1950, when its editors remarked that the translation employs '816 words . . he there used fifty, seventy-five, one hundred, and even three hundred years before the first use of these words . . recorded in the *OED*', in addition to the 640 'first' instances already credited to him.

Skelton's impressive total of perhaps 1500 'first' usages is, in part, a matter of his coinciding with what the *OED* regards as the 'normalisation' of English in the sixteenth century, and in particular the consolidation of 'London' English as a national standard, at least for literary purposes, displacing the previous situation of comparative parity, and of formidable diversity of vocabulary, grammar and spelling systems, as between, say, Langland, the *Gawain* poet and

Chaucer.[4] Skelton's work comes at the very beginning of recognisably 'modern' English, as it takes its place in that privileged London literary-linguistic 'line' from Chaucer to Shakespeare; while at the same time it straddles and deliberately juxtaposes a variety of other classical and colloquial registers.

Mikhail Bakhtin's work may enable us to understand more precisely this historical location and condition of Skelton's work, and to recognise more fully the peculiar nature of his achievement, though this essay can only provide mere pointers to a Bakhtinian 're-reading'.[5]

Aspects of Bakhtin

Tri-lingualism fascinated Bakhtin. He constantly returns to the emergence of 'Latin' literature itself in the work of

> all the translator-stylisers who had come to Rome from lower Italy, where the boundaries of three languages and cultures intersected with one another—Greek, Oscan and Roman . . This literature was born in the inter-animation of three languages—one that was indigenously its own, and two that were other but that were experienced as indigenous. (p. 63)

This initiating confluence is indeed, for Bakhtin, a special case of the general condition of all language; the intimate

---

[4] For Skelton's 'first' usages, cf. Skelton (1957), vol II., pp. xxxii-xxxiii, and Salter (1946), pp. 119-217. For the general history cf. e.g. Leith (1983), chs 1 and 2

[5] Bakhtin's main works available in translation are *Problems of Dostoievsky's Poetics* (1963); *Rabelais and his World* (1965); and *The Dialogical Imagination*, essays edited by Michael Holquist. Quotations from Bakhtin in this essay are taken from *The Dialogical Imagination*, to which page references are given. See Todorov (1984) and Clark and Holquist (1984) for the debate on Bakhtin's possible authorship of works published under the names Voloshinov and Medvedev.

inter-animation of 'languages", of *polyglossia* and *heteroglossia*. What concerns Bakhtin is not only Greek Oscan Roman (or Latin French English) but 'the language of the cadet, the high-school student, the trade-school student'; 'every age group has its own language, its own vocabulary, its own particular accentual system'; 'even languages of the day exist: today's and yesterday's socio-ideological and political "day" do not, in a certain sense, share the same language: every day represents another socio-ideological semantic "state of affairs". '

> At any given moment of its historical existence, language is heteroglot from top to bottom: it represents the co-existence of socio-ideological contradictions between the present and the past, between differing epochs of the past, between different socio-ideological groups in the present, between tendencies, schools, circles and so forth, all given a bodily form. (p. 291)

Bakhtin's emphasis allows him to assert afresh an insight of Ferdinand Bruno, the historian of the French language:

> . . the very attempt of the Renaissance to establish the Latin language in all its classical purity inevitably transformed it into a dead language. It was impossible to sustain the classical Ciceronian purity of language while using it in the course of everyday life. . . The re-establishment of a classically pure Latin restricted its area of application to essentially the sphere of stylization alone. . . At the same time classical Latin illuminated the face of medieval Latin. This face, as it turned out, was hideous; but this face could only be seen in the light of classical Latin. (p. 80)

It is through this double disqualification that a contemporary 'vernacular' can assume an independent status. For Bakhtin the Renaissance moment of transition to national *vernacular* standards is one crucial instance of the repeated, permanent 'struggle between two tendencies in the languages of European peoples: one a centralizing (unifying) tendency, the other a de-centralizing tendency (that is, one that stratifies languages)' (p. 67). Out of that moment, the modern 'novel' emerges:

> The literary-artistic consciousness of the modern novel, sensing itself on the border between two languages, one literary, the other extra-literary, each of which now knows heteroglossia, also senses itself on the border of time: it is extraordinarily sensitive to time in language. (p. 67)

One thinks again of Skelton's 1500 'new' words. What characterises the 'novel' (for Bakhtin a much wider term than in normal usage) is polyphony, double-voicedness, the dialogical use of 'languages': 'every novel is a dialogized system made up of the images of "languages", styles and consciousnesses that are concrete and inseparable from language' (p. 49).

> Heteroglossia, once incorporated into the novel (whatever the form of its incorporation), is another speech in another's language, serving to express authorial intentions but in a refracted way. It serves two speakers at the same time and expresses simultaneously two different intentions: the direct intention of the character who is speaking, and the refracted intention of the author. In such discourse there are two voices, two meanings, and two expressions. And all the while these two voices are dialogically related; . . it is as if they actually hold a conversation with each other. Double-voiced discourse is always internally dialogized. (p. 324)

It is time to return to Skelton. A detailed Bakhtinian reading of his whole *oeuvre* is beyond the scope of this essay, but by juxtaposing these and other passages from Bakhtin with some introductory comments on Skelton's poems, I hope to suggest fruitful ways of 'reading' this body of work produced on the very brink of the English 'Renaissance'.

Skelton was born about 1460, probably graduated from Cambridge in 1480, and in 1488 received the title of 'Laureate' (indicating qualifications in Rhetoric) from Oxford. The same year he entered royal service at the Court of the recently victorious Henry VII, and throughout the 1490s was apparently tutor to Prince Arthur and Prince Henry. In that capacity he wrote a brief handbook of advice for princes (*Speculum Principis*, first published in 1934) and several pedagogical works (now lost), including a Grammar. But by 1502 Arthur was dead, and Skelton seems to have been retired as tutor, becoming Rector of Diss, a country parish near Norwich. Despite his pleading overtures when Henry VIII succeeded to the throne in 1509, Skelton did not return to Court office until 1513, when he assumed the title Orator Regius. His contemporaries and acquaintances included More, Erasmus, Wyatt and Surrey as well as such figures as Stephen Hawes, Alexander Barclay and Dunbar. He died in 1529, just as the issue of the King's divorce broke surface and with it the beginnings of the Henrican Reformation.[6]

Thus, after his academic years of scholarship and translating, Skelton spent two periods at Court, with a spell as a country vicar between, and some of his poems can clearly be linked to these different social environments. The Court poems from both periods include some obviously 'official' pieces, in Latin and English, celebrating military victories, lamenting royal deaths and castigating national enemies. He also wrote a competent and substantial Morality play, *Magnyfycence*,[7] for the court's edification and, for the King's amusement, contributed scathing diatribes to a number of 'flytings', *Against Dundas* and *Agenst Garnesche* (quoted earlier)—the Billingsgate language of each outburst

---

[6] For biographical information on Skelton, cf. Nelson (1939); Gordon (1943); Edwards (1949); Pollet (1971).

[7] The play is included in Happé (1979), and there is a critical edition by Neuss (1980). Cf. also Harris (1965).

against Garnesche is concluded with 'By the kyngys most noble commaundemennt'.

But the most intriguing of his Court poems is itself a critique of court life, bringing together, and freshly enlivening, a number of long-conventional satiric devices. *The Bouge of Court* (bouge means rations or reward) was written c. 1498, at Henry VII's court. Skelton uses the dream convention to dramatise a nightmare of court intrigue. The dreamer, and victim, is a persona but one not easily distinguished from Skelton: a man of learning, a scholar, somewhat marginal to the court, neither lord nor administrator, neither soldier nor prelate; his position makes him both vulnerable and, perhaps, potentially powerful. He is aboard the Ship of Court (and of fools?) and his name is significant: Drede—dread, fear, uncertainty, unsureness. Yet at first there is nothing specific to be afraid of. On the contrary, the other courtiers seem only too friendly. But if their names, and their number—seven: Favell (flattery), Suspycyon, Hervy Hafter (swindler), Disdayne, Ryote, Dyssymulation and Disceyre—do not warn us, what they say should. First, Flavell to Drede:

> Ye be an apte man, as ony can be founde
> To dwell with us and serve my ladyes grace.
> Ye be to her, yea, worth a thousande pounde.
> I herde her speke of you within shorte space,
> Whan there were dyverse that sore dyde you manace.
> And, though I say it, I was myselfe your frende,
> For here be dyverse to you that be unkynde. ...
> Farewell tyll soone. But no word that I sayde:
> (155-61, 175).

But then Drede overhears this same Favell speaking with Suspycyon:

> 'In fayth,' quod Suspecte,'spake Drede no worde of me?'
> 'Why? What than? Wylte thou lete men to speke?
> He sayth he can not well accorde with the.'
> 'Twyst,' quod Suspecte, 'goo playe; hym I ne reke!'
> 'By Cryste,' quod Favell, 'Drede is soleyne freke!

What, lete us holde him up, man, for a whyle.'
'Ye, soo,' quod Suspecte, 'he may us bothe begyle.'
(183-9)

Yet Suspycyon's first words to Drede are:

'Ye remembre the gentylman ryghte nowe
That commaunde with you, me thought, a praty space?
Beware of him, for I make God avowe,
He wyll begyle you and speke fayre to your face.
Ye never dwelte in suche an other place,
For here is none that dare well other truste;
But I wolde telle you a thynge, and I durste.
Spake he, a fayth, no worde to you of me?
I wote, and he dyde, he wolde me telle.'
(197-205)

After this Hervy Hafter sidles up, with some even more intricate advice, before going off for a whispered conversation with Disdayne, who then comes over to Drede and angrily accuses him:

'Remembrest thou what thou sayd yesternyght?
Wylt thou abyde by the wordes agayne?'
(325-4)

Although Disdayne and Drede have not met before, Disdayne is claiming that Drede said something to him (or to someone else) the previous night and that Disdayne knows about it and resents it; but what it is that Drede is alleged to have said neither he nor the reader ever discovers. Dyssymulation further increases this sense of paranoid backstairs whispering and tale-bearing, while (of course) deploring it to Drede. The climax comes when Disceyte slinks up to Drede with yet more obscure messages, rumours and reports, culminating in a veiled warning that Drede is in great danger (512-25). At this Drede finally loses whatever courage he has left:

And as he rounded thus in myne ere
Of false collusyon confetryd by assente,
Me thoughte I see lewde felawes here and there
Came for to slee me of mortall entente.
And as they came, the shypborde faste I hente
And thoughte to lepe; and even with that woke,
Caught penne and ynke, and wrote this lytell boke.
(526-52)

What Skelton is presenting, dramatising, in the poem is the complex and threatening atmosphere of a court in which the main weapon against others is language itself, a bewildering cross-current of speech and alleged speech, rumour and accusation, calumny and lying. Caught at the centre of these whirlpools of half-understood whisperings and overheard plottings, Drede's nerve finally cracks. By the end of the poem he is no longer sure of what has been said about him, or to whom, or even what he has said himself. Any move he makes may be misinterpreted; any ally he finds might be betraying him behind his back; any advice he trusts may be a device to ensnare him. He opts out. He simply leaps over the side, in an act of suicide—and thereby wakes up.

Yet the leap is a curious one: he jumps out of his dream, but only to awaken, presumably, in the same kind of court situation that the poem has depicted. The poet, like Drede, is a courtier too. And the final stanza makes it clear that in the real court of Henry VII language is similarly open to interpretation and mis-interpretation: words remain as weapons, and the poem itself may be used against him.

I wolde therwith no man were myscontente;
Besechynge you that shall it see or rede,
In every poynte to be indyfferente,
Syth all in substaunce of slumbrynge doth precede.
I wyll not saye it is mater in dede,
But yet oftyme suche dremes be founde trewe.
Now constrewe ye what is the resydewe.
(533-9)

Skelton here is beginning to explore what will become a central problem for him: how, as a poet, he can use words to tell the truth in a situation where words are dangerous weapons, even for their user. And he has done so in a form which closely matches Bakhtin's notion of the dialogic novel. Not only is much of the poem constructed in actual dialogues, but the inter-animation of distinct 'voices' creates a double structure: at one level, a conspiracy of courtiers converging upon a central protagonist, Drede; at another, a de-centred series of implicit relations between the seven deadly courtiers themselves, in which each is both practitioner and victim of his own and others' characteristic courtly vices. The resulting narrative is genuinely 'novelistic', in Bakhtin's extended sense.

Three 'Love' Poems

In his study of humanism and poetry at the court of Henry VIII, H. A. Mason offers a comparison between 'the delicacy of Wyatt's poise' and the 'ludicrous attempt' in Skelton's 'The auncient acquaintance, madam, betwen us twayn', 'to preserve a courtly tone of politeness' (Mason, 1959, p. 189). Yet if we read the poem (p. 42), in a Bakhtinian rather than Leavisite frame of mind, it is certainly *not* an 'attempt to preserve a courtly tone of politeness' on the poet's part that will strike us, but rather the sharp and deliberately humorous clash between the 'refined' Latinate vocabulary and over-polite tones of the first two stanzas and the colloquial, sexually-charged 'horsey' (or whore-sy?) terms and rhythms of the succeeding stanzas.

It is the very excess of involvement with 'madam's' sexual energies, registered in the language, that retrospectively turns the satire against the speaker. It is curdled jealousy and wounded lust, not moral indignation or sympathy for an abused husband, that really speaks: the 'I' has also been 'your old, trew, loving knyght' (another horseman) in that 'former dalyaunce', and we find ourselves registering the ornate compliments of the opening as barely concealed inducements to join in the imagined orgies to come, while the violence of the ''jentyll' husband disposes us to side with the pleasure-seeking wife and finally to concur with the advice to her, not to abstain from but simply to conceal more effectively ('warke more secretly') her affairs.

The opening and closing tones of the poem are destabilised and subverted by the explosion of a quite 'other' language at the centre of the poem, yet, noticeably, that language is itself another 'language' of the 'I' in which is imagined the lusty cries of 'madam' and her lovers. In the relation between these two languages there is even an echo of today's officers' mess: that revealing combination of, and sudden slide between, refinement and rectitude, chauvinist crudity and brutality, which perhaps always shadows the overt codes of 'knightly'chivalry.

In 'Manerly Margery Mylk and Ale' (p. 35), as Stanley Fish has argued (1965, lines 42-6), we need to insert quotation marks at various points to establish the contributions of two speakers, in a dialogue of a traditional kind between 'serving maid' and 'clerk'. But in order to distribute the lines confidently we probably need a finer aural discrimination between fifteenth century social languages than present knowledge allows us. Or, quite plausibly, Skelton has deliberately constructed a poem which allows a variety of possible dialogical performances, a variable orchestrating not only of overt sexual responses but also of male-female power relations. (Some medieval poems can be punctuated variously to yield either a social 'complaint' or a Utopian celebration.) But certainly the play of the poem is the effect of a constant relay between 'languages' which gives 'bodily shape' to the relations between two interacting social representatives in a dramatic present, while the refrain may well add a third 'voice', in a coarsely earthy idiom which can be appropriated by either speaker or by the narrating poet.

'My darlyng dere' (p. 41) offers a more complex play between languages and attitudes, since the opening refrain,

With 'lullay, lullay', lyke a chylde,
Thou slepyst to long, thou art begylde!

deploys a register of affectionate gentleness that the poem initially sustains in the lovers' dialogue, only to undermine it, remorselessly ending with an explicit address by the narrating voice that wholly punctures the superficially sympathetic tones of the rest:

> What dremyst thou, drunchard, drousy pate?
> Thy lust and lykyng is from the gone;
> Thou blynkerd blowboll, thou wakyst to late;
> Behold, thou lyeste, luggard, alone! . .
> I wys, powle hachet, she bleryd thyne I!

In their use of distinctly 'low' language and vivid ventriloquism, these poems may be linked with 'Womanhod, wanton, ye want' (p. 40), addressed to 'Mastres Anne' who lived at 'The Key' in Thames Street (an inn? a brothel?), and the marvellously rumbustious and rightly famous 'The Tunnyng of Elynour Rummynge' (p. 214). To move from these to, say, the ornate elegance of 'Knowledge, aquayntance, resort, favour, with grace' (p. 43) or the finely poised tributes to the ladies of the Howard family, in 'The Garlande of Laurell' (pp. 335-43), is to realise the range of social languages Skelton could deploy within his verse, the potential for linguistic inter-animation available to him.

Church poems

One crucial social language was that of the Church, and a number of the poems after Skelton's ordination, in 1498, are relatively straightforward in their parodic and goliardic use of ecclesiastical Latin and liturgical phrasing. The 'Devoute Trentale for old John Clarke, sometyme the holy patriarke of Dis' (p. 106) records, for example, that:

> *In parochia de dis*
> *Non erat sibi similis*
> *In malicia vir insignis*
> *Duplex corde et bilinguis*
> *Senio confectus*
> *Omnibus suspectus*

Nemini dilectus.
Sepultus est amonge the wedes
God forgeve hym his mysdedes.

(In the parish of Diss / Was no one like this / A man renowned for malice / Fork-tongued and treacherous / Consumed by senility / Mistrusted by everybody /Beloved by nobody / Buried he is among the weeds / God forgive him his misdeeds.)

And so on, for 90 lines! Adam Uddersale, 'the holy bailiff of Dis', is given a similarly 'devout' epitaph. But the interplay between liturgy and satire is less easy to decipher in two major poems 'Philip Sparrow' and 'Ware the Hawk'.

The ostensible situation in 'Ware the Hawk' is simple enough: a "lewde curate, / A parson benyfyced' has been discovered by Skelton exercising his hunting hawks within the church at Diss and the poem is (apparently) an all-out attack on this dastardly sacrilege. A picture of sheer mayhem is conjured up: one hawk devours a pigeon on the altar itself; a second perches on the rood loft, is enticed down with meat and bludgeoned into insensibility; the parson threatens to bring his hounds in and chase foxes through the sanctuary; he overturns

my offerynge box,
Boke, bell and candyll,
All that he myght handyll;
Cros, staffe, lectryne and banner,
Fell downe on thys manner.
(111-15)

A slanging-match follows in which the parson

wysshed withall
That the dowves donge
Downe myght fall
Into my chalys at mas,
When consecrated was
The blessyd sacrament
(182-6)

Skelton finally takes it upon himself to castigate this polluter of holy places, in an extraordinary rhetorical diatribe:

> Of no tyrand I rede,
> That so far dyd excede;
> Neither yet Dyoclesyan,
> Nor yet Domysyan;
> Nother crokyd Cacus,
> Nor yet dronken Bacus
> Nother Olybryus,
> Nor Dyonysyus;
> Nother Phalary,
> Rehersyd in Valery,
> Nor Sardanapall,
> Unhappyest of all;
> Nor Nero the worst,
> Nor Clawdyus the curst;

and so on, ending with:

> nor the Turke,
> Wrought never such a worke,
> For to let their hawkys fly
> In the church of Saynt Sophy;
> With moch matter more
> That I kepe in store.
> (190-221)

Given that Skelton must have known of the actual plundering of Hagia Sophia when the Turks took Constantinople in 1453, this final assertion that at least they didn't fly hawks in the place (they merely slaughtered several thousand Christians) is the last straw in this crazy catalogue of comparative (and often madly inappropriate) outrage.

By this stage our composite image of Skelton spluttering and fulminating amidst the wreckage of his church, with bloodied hawks flying around, foxes leaping for cover, pigeons shitting in the chalice, is surely irresistibly funny. And the final section of the poem takes the absurdities even further, with a ludicrous Latin cryptogram (which defied decipherment till 1896) which the parson (and the baffled reader?) is ridiculed for not understanding! The culminating accusation might well be turned against Skelton himself:

> This dowtless ye ravyd
> Dys church ye thus depravyd;.
> *Quare? Quia evangelia*
> *Concha et conchelia*
> *Accipiter et sonalia*
> *Et bruta animalia*
> *Cetera quoque talia*
> *Tibi sunt equalia.* (307-16)

> (Why? Because the holy gospels / The vestments and the vessels / The hunter and its bells / And senseless animals / And everything else too / Are all the same to you.)

The effect of this extraordinary organisation of rhetorical ploys is to make us laugh at the exaggerated inappropriateness and extravagance of Skelton's cantankerous reaction—all this because a hawk was exercised in his church! And yet, precisely within the framework of a deeply-held conviction of the real presence of Christ Himself within the sacramental celebration, such desecration is truly more horrendous than any offence within the purely human range, is in a different category of sin altogether. Nevertheless, the interplay of endorsement and implicit mockery of this belief, of serious outrage and irreverent fun, produces in the poem as a whole an ambivalence of attitude beyond mere parody; precisely a sense of 'an unconcluded dialogue between ideological attitudes' (Bakhtin) which the reader has to resolve. As Bakhtin remarked: 'The author participates in the novel (he is omnipresent in it) with almost no direct language of his own. The language of the novel is a system of languages that mutually and ideologically interanimate each other' (p. 47).

The same comment applies even more to 'Philip Sparrow', a marvellous 1400-line poem which falls clearly but intriguingly into two main sections and ''voices'. In the first 800 lines a young girl, Jane, laments her dead sparrow, killed by a convent cat. This first half has been generally praised for the vivid picturing of the bird itself; the structural device of linking its various sections according to patterned Latin phrases from the liturgical office for the dead; the magnificent curse upon cats uttered by Jane; the delightful idea, pursued in detail, of all the other birds performing the various liturgical roles in a mass for the dead sparrow. But, above all, readers have warmed to the persona of Jane herself, her naivety, her innocence, her adolescent half-learning, her genuine sorrow. By a delicate interweaving of naive emotional response and solemn liturgical resonance, a vivid presence is created, an audible voice, a palpable presence:

> It had a velvet cap,
> And wold syt upon my lap,
> And seke after small wormes,
> And somtyme white bred crommes;
> And many tymes and ofte
> Betwene my brestes softe
> It wolde lye and rest—
> It was propre and prest.
> Somtyme he wolde gaspe
> Whan he sawe a waspe;
> A fly, or a gnat,
> He wolde flye at that;
> And prytely he wolde pant
> Whan he saw an ant;
> Lord, how he wolde pry
> After the butterfly!
> Lorde, how he wolde hop
> After the gressop!
> And when I sayd, 'Phyp, Phyp,'
> Than he wold lepe and skyp,
> And take me by the lyp.
> Alas, it wyll me slo,
> That Phillyp is gone me fro!
> *Si in i qui ta tes*
> Alas, I was evyll at ease!

De pro fun dis cla ma vi,
When I sawe my sparowe dye! (120-46)

The whole first part seems a gently sympathetic portrayal of the young girl, touched lightly with humour and psychological insight. The verse is simple, open, moving.

But a change comes in the second part. Jane finally tries to compose an epitaph for her sparrow, not in 'Myne Englyssh halfe-abused' but in 'Latyne playne and lyght', at which point a second voice intervenes and takes over, that of 'laureate poet Skelton':

Flos volucrum formose, vale!
Philippe, sub isto
Marmore iam recubas,
Qui mihi carus eras.
Semper erunt nitido
Radiantia sydera celo;
Impressusque meo
Pectore semper ens.
Per me laurigerum
Britanum Skeltonida vatem
Hec cecinisse licet
Ficta sub imagine texta.
Cuius ens volucris,
Prestanti corpore virgo:
Candida Nais erat,
Formosior ista Joanna est:
Docta Corinna fuit,
Sed magis ista sapit.
Bien men souvient. (826-44)

(Flower of birds most beautiful, farewell! / Philip, beneath that / Marble now you rest / Who to me was dear. / Always there will be / Radiant stars in the bright sky; / Always you will be / Imprinted on my heart. / Through this laureated one / Brittanic Poet Skelton / These made-up songs could sing / By my imagining: / She whose bird you were / Is a maiden past compare: / Nympho was fair, / This Jane's a stunner! / Corinna was clever, /But Jane's an all-round winner! / How well I remember!)

The effect of these lines is to set up a whirligig of levels of reality: 'Jane' laments the dead bird while Skelton lauds the live girl. But the Jane who laments is a fiction of Skelton's (even if there was a real Jane) so the Jane he drools over is (for us at least) the product of his own imagination—as indeed is the sparrow so persuasively created for the reader in the fictional Jane's sorrow. By acknowledging the constructed character of the first part, the status of the second part is also thrown into question, since what follows is an apparently blasphemous appropriation of liturgical praise of the Virgin Mary to celebrate Skelton's patently lustful regard for the girl. And yet that persona is also signalled as playfully deliberate:

> Lorde, how I was payned!
> Unneth I me refrayned,
> How she me had reclaymed,
> And me to her retayned,
> Enbrasynge therewithall
> Her goodly myddell small
> With sydes longe and streyte;
> To tell you what conceyte
> I had than in a tryce,
> The matter were to nyse,
> And yet there was no vyce,
> Nor yet no vyilany,
> But only fantasy. (1125-35)

> Her kertell so goodly lased,
> And under that is brased
> Such pleasures that I may
> Neyther wryte nor say;
> Yet though I wryte not with ynke,
> No man can let me thynke,
> For thought hath lyberte,

Thought is franke and fre. (1194-1201)[8]

We are unavoidably drawn back to apparently naive and coyly innocent moments in Jane's own words, and recognise Skelton's leer behind them:

For it wold come and go,
And fly so to and fro;
And on me it wolde lepe
Whan I was aslepe,
And his fethers shake,
Wherewith he wolde make
Me often for to wake
And for to take him in
Upon my nakyd skyn.
God wot, we thought no syn—
What though he crept so lowe?
.. Phyllyp, though he were nyse,
In him it was no vyse;
.. Phyllyp myght be bolde
And do what he wolde (159-78)

We can sense running through the poem an implicit wish-fulfilling identification of 'Skelton' with 'Philip' and a far from innocent knowingness both attributed to and denied of Jane. And when the whole poem ends with an 'addicyon' ostensibly rebutting 'Jane''s own complaints about the bad taste of the poem, we recognise that this too may be a further manipulation of personae.

The double- (or triple)-voiced character of 'Philip Sparrow' should be apparent. Not only are different registers of language deployed (liturgical, rhetorical, erotic, elegaic) but the 'voice' that speaks the whole poem is that of a Skelton who superbly constructs a 'Skelton' who imagines a 'Jane' who conjures up a 'Philip' who is a substitute for 'Skelton' — and each of these layers of persona has its appropriate tone, vocabulary and voice. And at work in it

---

[8] A nice instance of Skelton's playing with the rhetorical tradition; his model and target here is Geoffrey de Vinsauf's *Poetria Nova* (c.1210).

overall, as in 'Ware the Hawk', is a contradictory relation to religious attitudes, practices and norms, registered in the complex dialogisation of languages. Bakhtin again:

> Double-voiced discourse is always internally dialogized. Examples of this would be comic, ironic or parodic discourse, the refracting discourse of a narrator, refracting discourse in the language of a character and finally the discourse of a whole incorporated genre. . . A potential dialogue is embedded, . . one as yet unfolded, a concentrated dialogue of two voices, two world views, two languages. (p. 324)

Against Wolsey

Arguably, Skelton's most complex and brilliant poem is 'Speak, Parrot' which almost defies brief commentary and even defeats quotation. One stanza has already been quoted. Another sample:

Ic dien serveth for the estrych fether,
Ic dien is the language of the land of Beme;
In Affryc tongue byrsa is a thonge of lerher;
In Palestina there is Jerusalem.
Collustrum now for Parot, whyte bred and swete creme!
Our Thomasen she doth trip, our Jenet she doth shayle;
Paror hath a blacke beard and a fayre grene tayle.
(78-84)

Much of the first third of the poem is written like this. Some things, at least, are clear: the main speaker, being a parrot, chatters and chatters in various languages (since parrots have no linguistic nationality, or national loyalty). A parrot, of course, merely chatters: he doesn't *mean* anything of what he says, and he chatters in unconnected fragments, a kind of nonsense. But a parrot, in myth, is also a bird of paradise, speaking with the tongues of angels as well as speaking in tongues: he prophesies, speaks the real truth in veiled fashion. He is also immortal, so his historical memory is a long one: he can draw parallels with the present from even the more obscure of olden times. But he is also a ladies' pet, so he chatters for reward, for food, delicacies and affection, and the reward may mean more to him than the chatter—if the chatter means anything at all.

Yet every line of the quoted stanza does indeed make sense, and very specific sense. As various scholars have shown,[9] the poem constitutes a critical comment on Cardinal Wolsey's negotiations at the Calais conference in 1521. Wolsey was at this point Henry's most powerful minister and a major figure on the European scene, but his father had allegedly been a butcher, hence the references to 'colostrum' (the milk got at first calving) and to leather. 'Ich dien', 'I serve', was the royal motto, as the ostrich plume was the royal emblem, but (the poem suggests) the royal ostrich has put its head in the sand, not realising that the motto is becoming literally true: the King himself is serving, being manipulated by, the King's servant, Wolsey, who may well be serving the interests of Charles V, Emperor of 'Beme' (Bohemia), instead. 'In Affryc tongue *byrsa* is a thonge of lether': it is (in Renaissance lexicons) but in English usage 'burse', 'purse', means treasury; the 'Affryc' Queen, Dido, used the trick of measuring out land using a square yard of leather cut into narrow strips and laid end to end to claim more than was bargained for: Wolsey is milking the treasury by similarly dubious devices. And in 1518 he had negotiated yet another abortive treaty, committing England, France and Spain to a new crusade—but Jerusalem was still in the hands of the Turks.

Of course, this use of language *obscures* the attack embedded in it: it is almost indecipherable. Contemporary readers may have found it slightly clearer, but I doubt whether any reader ever found this part of the poem lucid. And that is part of the point. The Parrot wants to speak (it is a regular refrain in the poem) but only if he can get away with it. And the temptation is not to speak at all, to retreat into a pampered security, paring his toenails and enjoying his own mythic virility:

---

[9] Cf. works cited in note 6 above, and Brownlow (1971).

Parrot, Parrot, Parrot, praty popigay!
With my beke I can pyke my lyttel praty too;
My delyght is solas, pleasure, dysporte and pley;
Lyke a wanton, whan I wyll, I rele to and froo.
(106-9)

Yet the movement of the poem denies these options: eventually Parrot is forced to speak out.

The middle part of the poem is a complex dialogue between Parrot and Galathea (the name, incidentally, of Pygmalion's statue which finally found its human voice). Each exchange is given a specific date within the poem which apparently refers to the detailed stages of Wolsey's negotiations between August and November,—and which remind us of Bakhtin's remark that 'even languages of the day exist'. At last, Galathea, by referring (still obscurely) to Wolsey's alleged plan to make himself Pope, finally persuades Parrot:

Nowe, Parott, my swete byrde, speke owte yet ons agayn,
Sette asyde all sophysms, and speke now trew and playne.

There then follows, in a total shift of gear, a long, perfectly clear and direct general satire on every aspect of the contemporary scene:

So many morall maters, and so lytell usyd;
So myche newe makyng, and so madd tyme spente;
So myche translacion into Englyshe confused;
So myche nobyll prechyng, and so lytell amendment;
So myche consultacion, almoste to none entente;
So myche provision, and so lytell wytte at nede—
Syns Dewcalyons flodde there can no clerkes rede.
(449-55)

Parrot has at last found courage to speak. After ten similar stanzas the poem ends triumphantly:

Dixit, quod Parrot
Crescet in immensem me vivo Psitacus iste.
Hinc mea dicetur Skeltonidis inclita fama.
Quod Skelton Lawryat
Orator Regius

But it is not quite as simple as that. The diatribe that ends the poem is clear, lucid, intelligible, critical, angry—but it is general, a traditional lament for the times, a well-written, forceful example of an old genre. It therefore lacks all the specificity, the detailed allusions to Wolsey, and to precise political manipulations and occasions, that the first part included but obscured. As with 'Philip Sparrow', we have to take both parts together, as indicating now not just a deliberate ambivalence but a desperate problem. To speak out 'plainly' against Wolsey at the very height of his power—Cardinal Legate, Archbishop of York, Lord Chancellor, intermediary between Kings, Emperors and Popes—would be suicidal, and we are all partly cowards. Skelton will speak out against Wolsey and he will speak out plainly, but not both at the same time. And this is partly because it seems that his resources as a poet, the conventions available to him, can hardly allow him to. The 'general complaint' is a recognised genre; the obscure prophetic saying is an old political safety device. But how can he find a mode that combines the virtues of both, what language can he use?

Skelton's next poem, 'Collyn Clout', begins, in effect, with these problems:

What can it avayle . .
To ryme or to rayle,
To wryte or to indyte,
Other for delyte
Or elles for despyte?
Or bokes to compyle
Of dyvers maner style,
Vyce to revyle
And synne to exyle? . .

Or yf he speke playne,
Than he lacketh brayne:
'He is but a foole,
Let hym go to scole!'
(1-29)

'Colin Clout' finally adopts a far simpler and more direct language and style than the first part of 'Speke, Parrot', while being more detailed and specific than the second part. It depicts the various failings of the different social classes or 'degrees': the lack of learning, piety and responsibility in the clergy, the lack of authority in the nobility, the abdication of responsibility by the King. But where the style is simple, the structure of the poem and its political tactics are relatively sophisticated. Again, there is a persona, Colin Clout, lowly but honest, almost a peasant, one of a long line of spokesmen for the common man. Skelton uses Colin precisely as a reporter of other men's complaints. Colin endlessly reports 'what men say' —what the clergy say about the laity, what the laity say about the clergy, what they both say about the general state of society, for which the King is ultimately responsible.

It is a useful tactic, since each kind of critic can be used to belabour someone else, but is in turn criticised: his opinions are endorsed, implicitly, but his own actions judged, while Colin himself can escape censure since he offers himself as merely relating these criticisms in order for them to be refuted. But, of course, the device is also a transparent one, and since so many of these 1300 lines of barbed and bitter 'reportage' could certainly have a particular application to Wolsey himself, Skelton could have been under no illusion as to the possible reaction—and he boldly includes that reaction within the poem itself, in the very tones of Wolsey's alleged behaviour in Star Chamber proceedings:

'How daresr thou, daucocke, mell?
Howe darest thou, losell,
Allygate the gospell

Agaynst us of the counsell?
Avaunt to the devyll of hell!

Take him, wardeyn of the Flete,
Set hym fast by the fete!
I say, lieutenaunt of the Toure,
Make this lurdeyne for to loure;
Lodge hym in Lytell Ease,
Fede hym with beanes and pease!
The Kynges Benche or Marshalsy,
Have hym thyder by and by!
The vyilayne preceth openly
And dedareth our vyilany.'
(1160-74)

The poem ends on a note of sad defiance:

Ah, pudet! Ah, miseret! Vetor hic ego pandere plura
Pro gemitu et lacrimis; Prestet peto premia pena.

[It's shameful! It's deplorable! I have to desist from disclosing more now / Because of my groans and my tears; I pray the prize will outweigh the penalty.]

With astonishing courage, Skelton did not stop there. In another lengthy attack he abandoned all personae and simply launched himself on Wolsey. 'Why Come Ye Nat to Courte?' maintains at first a play of voices. The question in the title is repeated and ambiguously addressed (to the poet; to the nobles appealed to in the opening lines; to the reader), and various responses, excuses and explanations are given. The questioning voice seeks out gossip about Court figures who are ducking their responsibilities, and news about contemporary events and scandals. But finally, the responding voice bursts our of this framework of prevarication and procrastination:

Ones yet agayne
Of you I wolde frayne
Why come ye nat to court?...
To whyche court?
To the kynges courte?
Or to Hampton Court? [*Wolsey's palace*]

Nay, to the kynges court!
The kynges courte
Shulde have the excellence;
But Hampton Court
Hath the preemynence!
And Yorkes Place,
With, 'My lordes grace',
To whose magnifycence
Is all the conflewence,
Sutys, and supplycacyons,
Embassades of all nacyons.
Strawe for lawe canon,
Or for lawe common,
Or for lawe cyvyll;
It shall be as he wyll.
(399-419)

Almost as if he were conducting another 'flyting' and Wolsey merely another greasy Garnesche—but this time in deadly and dangerous earnest—Skelton piles up accusations for nearly a thousand lines. A sample:

So he dothe undermynde
And suche sleyghtes dothe fynde,
That the kynges mynde
By him is subverted
(437-40)

To tell the trouth playnly,
He is so ambicyous,
So shamles and so vicyous,
And so supersticyous,
And so moche oblivyous

From whens that he came,
That he falleth into *Acidiam*,
Whiche truly to expresse,
Is a forgetfulnesse,
Or wylfull blyndnesse,
Wherwith the Sodomites
Lost theyr inward syghtes.
(460-71)

Now the same Cardynall is promoted,
Yet with lewde condicyons cotyd
As herafter ben notyd:
Presumcyon and vayne glory,
Envy, wrath, and lechery,
Covetys and glotony;
Slouthfull to do good,
Now frantick, now starke wode!
Shulde this man of suche mode
Rule the swerde of myght?
(570-80)

Yet whan he coke first his hat,
He said he knew what was what.
All justyce he pretended:
All thynges sholde be amended,
All wronges he wolde redresse,
All injuris he wolde represse,
All perjuris he wolde oppresse.
And yet, this gracelesse elfe,
He is perjured himselfe.
(1108-16)

The poem concludes with an 'Apostrophe to the citizens of London':

Excitat, en, asinus mulum, mirabile visu,
Calcibus! O vestro cives occurite asselo
Qui regnum regemque regit, qui vestra gubernat
Predia, divitias, nummos, gasas, spoliando!

(Look! the ass arouses the mule—a marvel to see / With his heels! Citizens! rise against your little ass / Who rules kingdom and king, who lords it over / Your lands, your wealth, your cash, your treasures —by sheer plunder!)

Skelton was eventually reconciled with Wolsey, and they found a common enemy in the emergent Lutheran heresies—'A Replycacion' is humbly dedicated to the Cardinal—but it is not surprising that Skelton was long reputed to have spent his final years in sanctuary.

Bakhtin, Stalin and Skelton

This essay has been partly shaped by reference to Bakhtin's notion of the dialogic 'novel', but Skelton's work could, obviously, be approached within several other frameworks. The elucidatory tools and preoccupations of traditional literary scholarship provide an indispensable aid to the comprehension of much of his work, as well as the necessary clarification of his biography, the canon of his poetry, and the generic conventions he utilised.[10]

From a quite different perspective, it is relatively easy to imagine a 'deconstructionist' reading of at least some of his work. An intriguing temptation along such lines would be provided by the enigmatic marginal glosses (of deliciously uncertain authorial status) found alongside some poems, and reproduced in Dyce's 1843 edition.

Another important context in which to locate Skelton would be the transition from a manuscript culture to a print culture, as Caxton's tribute indicates.[11] It would be possible to incorporate such a context within a more extended 'Bakhtinian' reading, elaborating also Skelton's relation to rhetoric, to the tension between aureate and plain diction, to

10 Cf. e.g. Fishman (1971), for a recent survey; Kinsman and Yonge (1967); Heiserman (1961).

11 For the general context, see. e.g. Chaytor (1945); Febvre and Martin (1958); Blake (1969); Eisenstein (1979). It would, obviously, be interesting to investigate the mode of distribution and extent of circulation of Skelton's anti-Wolsey writings.

the 'New Learning' and the Grammarians' War (important concerns in 'Speke, Parrot').

A rather different Bakhtinian reading might be developed, indebted more to his book on Rabelais and exploring Skelton's possible relation to a popular cultural ethos: the grotesque realism of 'Elynour Rummynge' or even the tradition of 'Merry Tales' strongly associated with Skelton (which bedevilled earlier biographers) might be central here. Yet this essay has not sought to impose or elaborate any tightly systematic application of Bakhtin. Why, then, the deliberate choice in this essay of Bakhtin as a partner in dialogue with Skelton?

An answer might begin with Bakhtin's own insistence upon considering actual utterances in social situations (cf. p. 292). For it is surely obvious that Bakhtin's own work has a hidden agenda, legible in the light of events in the Soviet Union in the late 1920s and 1930s. Bakhtin's emphasis upon the diversity and fruitful inter-animation of national and cultural languages opposes the drive towards Great Russian hegemony. His recognition of ramified social complexity, of the multitude of coexistent 'socio-ideological groups' and their variable contradictions, problematises any easily reductive and prematurely schematic class analysis. His own polyphonic personae (as himself, as 'Volosinov', as 'Medvedev'?) and the double-focused intent of his cultural analyses are, at one level, a tactical response to the difficulties and dangers of 'living in a time of translation'. It is worth recalling that Stalin joined the first Soviet government as Commissar for Nationalities in 1918 (and quickly abandoned the principles of his own 1913 pamphlet *Marxism and the Nationalities Question*) while almost his last substantial publication was *Concerning Marxism in Linguistics* (1950), in which he anticipated a single world language.

For Bakhtin, perhaps, all the emphases of his analyses—from the tensions of tri-lingualism to the conflict between carnival and centralisation—were unified by an 'impulse' against Stalinism, and his own tactics of survival reproduced some of the devices he charted. Meanwhile, his great literary contemporary, Mandelstam, died in a labour camp for directly addressing Stalin as a 'murderer' in an unpublished poem.

If, now, we think of Skelton, one contrast is clear enough. Whatever the truth of Skelton's depiction of Wolsey, he obviously saw himself as confronting an overweening centralisation of all power in one man, an illegitimate absolutism on an awesome scale.[12] Finally abandoning the protection of veiled, allusive, cryptic 'double-voiced' criticism, he attacked in the plainest possible terms. It is worth, in conclusion, comparing two quotations. Bakhtin wrote, in 1934-35:

> In Rabelais . . a parodic attitude toward almost all forms of ideological discourse—philosophical, moral, scholarly, rhetorical, poetic and in particular the pathos-charged forms of discourse (in Rabelais, pathos almost always is equivalent to lie)—was intensified to the point where it became a parody of the very act of conceptualising anything in language . . Rabelais taunts the deceptive human word by a parodic destruction of syntactic structures, thereby reducing to absurdity some of the logical and expressively accented aspects of words (for example, predication, explanations, and so forth). Turning away from language (by means of language, of course), discrediting any direct or unmediated intentionality and expressive excess (any 'weighty' seriousness). . . presuming that all language is conventional and false, maliciously inadequate to reality—all this achieves in Rabelais almost the maximum purity in prose. But the truth that might oppose such falsity receives almost no direct intentional and verbal expression in Rabelais, it does not receive its own word—it reverberates only in the parodic and unmasking accents in which the lie is present. (p. 309)

---

12 For Wolsey, see. e.g. Cavendish (1558); Pollard (1929); and Ferguson (1958). Also relevant are Russell (1969); Guy (1977); Green (1980).

The passage, characteristically, hovers between praise and critique. Bakhtin's descriptions of dialogical polyphony invariably appear to imply an evaluative endorsement—and, in his own context, perhaps rightly so.

But much of today's de-politicised concern with polyphonic, elliptical, allusive, multi-layered textuality, with instant deconstrucrion of all attempts at predication and explanation, runs the risk of undervaluing and even dismissing other priorities and, sometimes, necessities. A re-reading of Skelton which simply, and enjoyably, rediscovers 'Speke, Parrot' as an admirable precursor of *The Waste Land* or *Finnegans Wake* may easily ignore 'Why Come Ye Nat to Courte? ' and the firm affirmation of a writer's responsibility which underpins it. Skelton's own poetic credo is formulated in theological terms we need not subscribe to, but the 'impulse' of his impassioned declaration ought at least to (re-)enter the current dialogue:

We are kyndled in suche facyon
With hete of the Holy Gost,
Which is God of myghtes most,
That he our penne dothe lede,
And maketh in us suche spede
That forthwith we must nede
With penne and ynke procede,
Somtyme for affection,
Sometyme for sadde dyrection,
Somtyme for correction,
Somtyme under protection
Of pacient sufferance,
With sobre cyrcumstance,
Our myndes to avaunce
To no mannes anoyance.
Therfore no grevance,
I pray you, for to take,
In this that I do make
Agaynst these frenetykes,
Agaynst these lunatykes,
Agaynst these sysmatykes,
Agaynst these heretykes,

Now of late abjured,
Most unhappely ured;
For be ye wele assured,
That frensy nor jelousy
Nor heresy wyll never dye.
Sunt infiniti, sunt innumerique sophiste,
Sunt infiniti, sunt innumerique logiste,
Innumeri sunt philosophi, sunt theologique,
Sunt infiniti doctores, suntque magistri
Innumeri; sed sunt pauci rarique poete.

(*A Replycacion*, 382 ff.)

'But poets are few and rare.' Milton and Marvell, for example, would have agreed—both plain-speaking 'Puritans' who could also practise a veiled allusiveness when it seemed necessary. In our own context, of course, the heresies and dogmatism, the frenzies and fanaticism, the centralising tendencies of arrogant power and blind wilfulness, may all be somewhat different from those which Skelton or Bakhtin confronted. But faced with a modern Wolsey we might be glad of another Skelton.

Perhaps, though, we should give the final word—as if on Skelton, but also in simultaneous homage—to Bakhtin:

> The word, breaking through to its own meaning and its own expression across an environment full of alien words and variously evaluating accents, harmonizing with some of the elements in this environment and striking a dissonance with others, is able, in this dialogized process, to shape its own stylistic profile and tone. (p. 277)

*

References.

Aurner, N.S. (1965) *Caxton: Mirror of Fifteenth-Century Letters* (New York: Russell & Russell).
Bakhtin, M. M. (1981) *The Dialogical Imagination: Four Essays*, ed. Michael Holquist (Austin: University of Texas Press).
Blake, N. F. (1969) *Caxton and his World* (London: Andre Deutsch).
Brownlow, F. M. (1971) ' The Book compiled by Maister Skelton, Poet Laureate, called *Speake, Parrot* ', *English Literary Renaissance*, I, pp. 3-26.
Cavendish, George (1558) *The Life and Death of Cardinal Wolsey*, in *Two Early Tudor Lives*, ed. R. S. Sylvester and D. P. Harding (New Haven: Yale University Press; reprt. 1962).
Chaytor, H. J. (1945) *From Script to Print* (London: Sidgwick and Jackson; reprt. 1966).
Clark, K. and Holquist, M. (1984) *Mikhail Bakhtin* (Cambridge, Mass.: Harvard University Press).
Edwards, A. S .G. (ed.) (1981) *Skelton: The Critical Heritage* (London: Routledge & Kegan Paul).
Edwards, H. L R. (1949) *Skelton: The Life and Times of an Early Tudor Poet* (London: Jonathan Cape).
Eisenstein, E. (1979) *The Printing Press as Agent of Change* (Cambridge: Cambridge University Press).
Febvre, L and Martin, H.-J. (1958) *The Coming of the Book* (London: New Left Books: reprt. 1976).
Ferguson, C. W. (1958) *Naked to Mine Enemies* (Toronto: Little, Brown).
Fish S. E. (1965) *John Skelton's Poetry* (New Haven: Yale University Press).
Fishman, B. (1971) 'Recent Studies in Skelton', *English Literary Renaissance*, I, pp. 89-96.
Gordon, I. A. (1943) *John Skelton: Poet Laureate* (Melbourne UniversityPress).
Green, R. F. (1980) *Poets and Princepleasers* (Toronto: University of Toronto Press).
Guy,J. A. (1977) *The Cardinal's Court* (Brighton: Harvester).
Happé, P. (ed.) (1979) *Four Morality Plays* (Harmondsworth: Penguin Books).
Harris, W. O. (1965) *Skelton's Magnyfycence and the Cardinal Virtue Tradition* (Chapel Hill: University of North Carolina Press).
Heiserman, A. R. (1961) *Skelton and Satire* (Chicago: University of Chicago Press).
Jones R. F. (1953) *The Triumph of the English Language* (Stanford University Press).

Kinsman, R. S. and Yonge, T. (1967) *John Skelton: Canon and Census* (Renaissance Society of America, Bibliographies & Indexes no. 4).
Leith R. (1983) *A Social History of English.* (London: Routledge & Kegan Paul).
Mason, H. A. (1959) *Humanism and Poetry in the Early Tudor Period* (London: Routledge & Kegan Paul).
Nelson, W. (1939) *John Skelton, Laureate* (rprt. New York: Russell & Russell, 1964).
Neuss, P. (ed.) (1980) *John Skelton: Magnificence* (Manchester: Manchester University Press).
Pollet, M. (1962) *John Skelton: Poet of, Tudor England* (London: Dent; rprt. 1971).
Russell, J. G. (1969) *The Field of Cloth of Gold* (London: Routledge & Kegan Paul).
Salter, E. (1983) *Fourteenth-Century English Poetry* (London: Oxford University Press).
Salter, F. M. (1946) 'Skelton's Contribution to the English Language', *Transactions of the Royal Society of Canada*, XXXIX, section 2, pp. 119-217.
Skelton, J. (1957) *The Bibliotheca Historica of Diodorus Siculus translated by John Skelton*, ed. F. M. Salter and H. L. R. Edwards (Early English Text Society, Oxford University Press).
Skelton, J. (1983) *The Complete English Poems,* ed. J. Scattergood (Harmondsworth: Penguin Books).
Todorov, T. (1984) *Mikhail Bakhtin: The Dialogical Principle* (Manchester: Manchester University Press).

*

THE APPROPRIATION OF MILTON

> I said to people here at Cambridge: in the thirties you were passing severely limiting judgements on Milton and relatively favourable judgements on the metaphysical poets, which in effect redrew the map of seventeenth-century literature in England. Now you were, of course, making literary judgments—your supporting quotations and analysis prove it, but you were also asking about ways of living through a political and cultural crisis of national dimensions. On the one side, you have a man who totally committed himself to a particular side and cause, who temporarily suspended what you call literature, but not in fact writing, in that conflict. On the other, you have a kind of writing which is highly intelligent and elaborate, that is a way of holding divergent attitudes towards struggle or towards experience together in the mind at the same time. These are two possibilities for any highly conscious person in a period of crisis—a kind of commitment which involves certain difficulties, certain naivetés, certain styles; and another kind of consciousness, whose complexities are a way of living with the crisis without being openly part of it. I said that when you were making your judgments about these poets, you were not only arguing about their literary practice, you were arguing about your own at that time. The reaction to this was scandalized denial that anything so tainted could have entered into the critical process.

Raymond Williams's remarks, in an interview with the editors of *New Left Review* in 1977,[1] indicate one basic difficulty in tracing and assessing the impact of Milton on subsequent generations: the inextricability (however frequently disavowed) of political and literary judgments. Thirty years earlier, T. S. Eliot, reflecting upon his own and

---

[1] Raymond Williams, *Politics and Letters* (London, New Left Books, 1979), pp. 335-6. [See below.]

Samuel Johnson's criticisms of Milton, admitted the difficulty:

> The fact is simply that the Civil War of the seventeenth century, in which Milton is a symbolic figure, has never been concluded. The Civil War is not ended: I question whether any serious civil war ever does end. Throughout that period English society was so convulsed and divided that the effects are still felt. Reading Johnson's essay one is always aware that Johnson was obstinately and passionately of another party. No other English poet, not Wordsworth, or Shelley, lived through or took sides in such momentous events as did Milton; of no other poet is it so difficult to consider the poetry simply as poetry, without our theological and political dispositions, conscious and unconscious, inherited or acquired, making an unlawful entry.[2]

Eliot's curious final phrase anticipates the later 'scandalized denial' which Williams records, for what is at stake for Eliot as for those Cambridge critics is the very possibility of regarding 'the poetry simply as poetry'.[3] It is at least doubtful if Milton himself would have accepted Eliot's formulation, yet, ironically, Milton's own poetry has been perhaps the crucial reference-point, in England, for precisely that notion of 'poetry' as an activity sublimely separate from all other concerns. An investigation of that apparent paradox may link and illuminate the areas this essay proposes to explore: the influence of Milton upon later readers, his own conception of 'the poet', and the role of Milton's work in the development of that deeply ideological practice we now call 'literary criticism'.

The entangled history of the reception and reputation of Milton over three centuries obviously cannot be summarized

---

[2] T.S. Eliot, *On Poetry and Poets* (London, Faber & Faber, 1957), p. 148.

[3] Eliot makes this problem explicit in the 'Note' to section II of his 1929 essay on Dante, *Selected Essays* (London, Faber & Faber, 1961), pp. 269-70.

here,[4] but some significant continuities can be indicated. As Mark Pattison noted, in 1879,

> Milton's repute was the work of the Whigs. The first *edition de luxe* of *Paradise Lost* (1688) was brought out by a subscription got up by the Whig leader, Lord Somers . . It was the Whig essayist, Addison, whose papers in the *Spectator* (1712) did most to make the poem popularly known. In 1737, in the height of the Whig ascendancy, the bust of Milton penetrated Westminster Abbey, though, in the generation before, the Dean of that day had refused to admit an inscription on the monument erected to John Phillips, because the name of Milton occurred in it.[5]

One conservative response to this Whig adulation, already apparent in the 1690s, was to concede, even applaud, Milton's stature as author of *Paradise Lost* while counter-posing the poetry to the prose, as if either the poem redeemed the politics or the pamphlets merely spoiled our appreciation of the poet—as in the reactions of Oldys and Yalden respectively:

> The bard, who next the new-born saint addrest,
> Was Milton, for his wondrous poem blest;
> Who strangely found, in his Lost Paradise, rest.
> 'Great bard', said he, ' 'twas verse alone
> Did for my hideous crime atone,
> Defending once the worst rebellion.'[6]

---

4 Cf. for example, W.R. Parker, *Milton's Contemporary Reputation* (Ohio State University Press, 1940); *Milton: the Critical Heritage*, ed. J.T. Shawcross (London, Routledge & Kegan Paul, 1970); *Milton Criticism: Selections from Four Centuries*, ed. J. Thorpe (London, Routledge & Kegan Paul, 1951); *The Romantics on Milton*, ed. J.A. Wittreich (Cleveland/London, Case Western Reserve University Press, 1970); James G. Nelson, *The Sublime Puritan: Milton and the Victorians* (Madison, University of Wisconsin Press, 1963).

5 Mark Pattison, *Milton* (London, Macmillan, 1890), p. 217.

6 Alexander Oldys, 'An Ode by Way of Elegy on .. Mr Dryden' (1700), in Shawcross, op. cit., p. 124.

> These sacred lines with wonder we peruse,
> And praise the flights of a seraphic muse,
> Till the seditious prose provokes our rage,
> And soils the beauties of thy brightest page.[7]

Two centuries later, Pattison's own biography of Milton reproduces this divorce between the prose and the poetry on another level, in its explicit organization and in its basic preferences:

> Milton's life is a drama in three acts. The first discovers him in the calm and peaceful retirement or Horton, of which *L'Allegro*, *Il Penseroso*, and *Lycidas* are the expression. In the second act he is breathing the foul and heated atmosphere of party passion and religious hate, generating the lurid fires which glare in the battailous canticles of his prose pamphlets. The three great poems, *Paradise Lost*, *Paradise Regained*, and *Samson Agonistes*, are the utterance of his final period of solitary and Promethean grandeur.[8]

During the second act:

> He was writing not poetry but prose, and that most ephemeral and valueless kind of prose, pamphlets, extempore articles on the topics of the day. He poured out reams of them, in simple unconsciousness that they had no influence whatever on the current of events.[9]

Both Gamett and Raleigh soon criticized Pattison for perpetuating this split, but George Whiting, writing in 1939, still had to propose a connection between the pamphlets and *Paradise Lost* as if his were a novel and tentative suggestion:

---

[7] Thomas Yalden, 'On the Reprinting of Milton's Prose Works' (1698), in Shawcross, op. cit., p. 122.

[8] Pattison, op. cit., p. 14.

[9] Ibid., p. 169.

> Literary critics who ignore backgrounds and who insist upon treating poetry as merely an aesthetic product have as a rule neglected or condemned Milton's work and interests in the period from 1640 to 1658, which they regard as an unfortunate episode in the life of the poet. Even those who do not deplore his activities in this middle period and who regard his prose as a powerful but unbalanced expression of his genius often fail to observe any relationship between the prose and the later poems . . [nevertheless] It is probable that *Paradise Lost* . is related more intimately than has been realized not only to Milton's prose but also to the political-religious interests that engrossed the middle period.[10]

One might easily interpret Eliot's notorious recommendation, three years earlier, that *Paradise Lost* itself should be read twice, 'first solely for the sound, and second for the sense',[11] as yet another variation on this long-established divorce between the 'prose' and the 'poetry' in Milton.

Whiting's book, as a contribution to 'Milton scholarship', utilized the prose primarily as a quarry to elucidate the poems. The long lineage behind such scholarship stretches back to Patrick Hume's 'Annotations' of 1695,[12] and his almost unprecedented treatment of a near-contemporary text as if it were a Greek or Latin classic requiring and justifying scholarly commentary was followed by Bentley's 1732 edition of *Paradise Lost*, with a textual apparatus and

---

10 G.W. Whiting, *Milton's Literary Milieu* (University of North Carolina Press, 1939, reissued by Russell & Russell, New York, 1964), pp. 218-19.

11 *On Poetry and Poets*, p. 143

12 Cf. A. Oras, *Milton's Editors and Commentators from Patrick Hume to Henry John Todd, 1695-1801* (London, Oxford University Press, 1931). Some established 'scholarly' approaches to Milton have been usefully criticized in Robert M. Adams, *Ikon: John Milton and the Modem Critics* (New York, Cornell University Press, 1955), especially Chapters III and V. Pattison considered that 'An appreciation of Milton is the last reward of consummated scholarship', Milton, p. 215.

editorial attitude that again accorded the poem 'classical' status. By the late nineteenth century, *Paradise Lost* had become, quite literally, the equivalent of a Latin text within the educational practices of the public schools: the Clarendon Commission of 1864 recorded that, at Shrewsbury, 'fourth-formers who were excused from studying Ovid's *Fasti* were expected to memorize about twelve hundred lines from Milton.'[13] The Taunton Commission, a few years later, was told how pupils at a Liverpool school

> took passages from Milton, read them backwards and forwards, and put them into other order, and they were obliged to parse them and explain them. The same faculties were exercised there in construing Milton as in construing Latin. [14]

F. R. Leavis presumably had such educational practices at least partly in mind when he complained in 1936 that 'however admirable' Milton's own prose and verse written in Latin 'may be judged to be, to latinize in English is quite another matter, and it is a testimony to the effects of the "fortifying curriculum" that the price of Milton's latinizing should have been so little recognized. '[15]

Criticism of Milton's 'latinizing' goes back to Addison, and beyond,[16] but Addison's main contribution to Milton's reputation was, of course, to develop and popularize the emphasis of Dennis and others on Milton's 'sublimity", thereby bequeathing to the eighteenth century one of its key terms and dominant influences. It was not, however, only the argument—and the unusual length—of Addison's criticism in the *Spectator* articles that shaped eighteenth-century responses to Milton. By devoting his Saturday essays

---

[13] R.D. Altick, *The English Common Reader* (Chicago and London, University of Chicago Press, 1963), p. 181.

[14] Ibid., p. 185

[15] F.R. Leavis, *Revaluation* (Harmondsworth, Penguin), p. 50.

[16] T.S. Eliot, *On Poetry and Poets*, p. 153, quotes Samuel Johnson's 'most important censure of Milton', which in turn quotes Addison's phrase: 'Our language sunk under him. '

to Milton, Addison indicated and encouraged the suitability of *Paradise Lost* for Sunday reading,[17] and throughout the eighteenth and nineteenth centuries Milton's poem shared the privileged and widely influential status of 'Sunday book' with those other 'Puritan' texts, *Pilgrim's Progress* and *Robinson Crusoe.* Q.D. Leavis, lamenting in 1932 the demise of this domestic practice, commented:

> The difference that the disappearance of the Sunday book a generation ago has made, its effect on the outlook and mental capacity of the people, would repay investigation.[18]

A specific topic for investigation in the case of *Paradise Lost* is indicated by T. H. Huxley's complaint, recorded by Pattison, that deeply engrained popular conceptions of cosmogony, so resistant to scientific enlightenment, actually derived from *Paradise Lost* Book VII rather than from *Genesis* itself. Pattison himself claimed, even more radically yet quite convincingly, that 'most English men and women would probably have some difficulty in discriminating in recollection' what they had derived from Milton and what from the Bible concerning the whole story of the Creation and Fall.[19]

Yet it was not only ordinary households of an Evangelical cast which accorded *Paradise Lost* a special status. The various designations in the eighteenth century of Satan as the 'hero' of the poem, according to the 'rules' of epic, were transmuted by Blake and Shelley into a political reading of the poem which was inherited by the radical working class of the nineteenth century, while Milton's own political

---

17 A point made by Patrick Parrinder, *Authors and Authority: a Study of English Literary Criticism and its Relation to Culture 1750-1900* (London, Routledge & Kegan Paul, 1977), p. 11.

18 Q.D. Leavis, *Fiction and the Reading Public* (London, Chatto & Windus, 1932, 1968), p. 117.

19 Pattison. Milton, pp. 184, 189. Readers who experience this difficulty can now consult the excellent work by J.M. Evans, *Paradise Lost and the Genesis Tradition* (Oxford University Press, 1968).

commitment to the Commonwealth was re-emphasized in the context of Chartist struggles. The *Chartist Circular* for 13 March 1841 carried a glowing account of Milton as 'an honest, unflinching stern Republican', who 'valiantly fought for civil and religious liberty, against the tyranny of Charles I'; but it is worth noting that Milton's life and prose writings are given priority in the article over the poetry, with *Paradise Lost* summarized in a single paragraph.[20] The *Northern Star* for 5 July 1845 advertised twelve lectures by the recently imprisoned Thomas Cooper, beginning with 'Ancient Egypt' and ending with 'prospects of the future'; the entire ninth lecture was to be on 'Milton: his patriotism and poetry etc.'[21] Cooper himself records that he had, by the age of thirteen, 'read the "Paradise Lost"; but it was above my culture and learning, and it did not make me feel, though I read it with interest, as a mere story.'[22] One wonders how many working-class readers of, for example, the eighteen 'cheap serial' numbers of *Paradise Lost* published in 1825-6 had the same reaction. [23]

Clearly, these mere indicators of Milton's impact and reputation represent only a highly selective fragment of the whole, while the direct and indirect influence of Milton upon English literature is, obviously, pervasive and incalculable. [24] My examples, however, illustrate the extent to

---

[20] The essay is reprinted in *An Anthology of Chartist Literature*, ed. Y. V. Kovalev (Moscow, 1956), pp. 299-302. Cf. also A.K. Stevens, 'Milton and Chartism', *Philological Quarterly*, XII (1933), pp. 377-88.

[21] The advertisement is given in full in John Saville's Introduction to *The Life of Thomas Cooper Written by Himself* (1872) (Leicester University Press, 1971), pp.18-20.

[22] *The Life of Thomas Cooper Written by Himself* (London, Hodder & Stoughton, 1872), p. 35.

[23] Cf. Louis James, *Fiction for the Working Man 1830-1850* (Harmondsworth. Penguin University Books, 1974), p. 89. James notes (p. 113) that Milton even appeared as a character in J. F. Smith's 'immensely popular' penny issue historical novel *Stanfield Hall* (1849-50).

[24] Cf., for example, R.D. Havens, *The Influence of Milton on English Poetry* (Cambridge, Harvard University Press, 1922). For some

which Milton's work has been appropriated within each of the crucial social and ideological institutions of English society: educational, religious, domestic and political. That *Paradise Lost* should be memorized by public schoolboys, recommended to radical Chartists, selected as suitable Sunday reading by Christian households, applauded by Whig politicians and encased in scholarly commentaries, at least underlines its peculiar status. Some explanation of that extraordinary position might be approached by briefly considering Milton's own practice as a writer in relation to the social and ideological institutions of the seventeenth century.

Any summary of Milton's various pronouncements on the nature of a 'poet' and on his own conception of his 'calling' would result in a complexly over-determined definition, drawing upon elements inherited from or paralleled in Sidney, Spenser, Jonson and, behind them, Plato, Aristotle, Quintilian, Cicero, Horace and the Bible: the poet as orator, teacher, statesman, creator, prophet.[25] A different but complementary approach would recognize that almost every text, whether 'prose' or 'poetry', produced by Milton prior to the publication of *Paradise Lost* bears traces of some contextual situation, of a relationship to a postulated and particular audience within some social or institutional setting, and in many cases those traces indicate more than a merely textual convention.

When Milton constructs the *Areopagitica* as a classical oration delivered to 'the Parliament of England' or addresses himself to 'the Lords and Commons' in *The Doctrine and Discipline of Divorce*, the rhetorical device embodies a real social practice which the text transposes: Milton is, at one level, actually appealing to the Parliament as legislators who may indeed be persuaded. Even as late as February 1659 the

---

interesting indications of Milton's indirect influence upon a significant branch of English prose fiction see David Punter, *The Literature of Terror: a history of Gothic Fictions from 1765 to the present day* (London, Longman, 1980, *passim*).

25 There is a usefully compressed account by Isabel Rivers, 'The making of a seventeenth-century poet', *John Milton: Introductions*, ed. J. Broadbent (Cambridge University Press, 1973), pp. 75-107.

rhetorical gestures indicate a genuine and specific attempt at intervention:

> I have prepared, supreme Council, against the much expected time of your sitting, this treatise . . in a season wherein the timely reading thereof to the easier accomplishment of your great work may save you much labour and interruption. [26]

Similarly, a great deal of the poetry can be assigned to particular occasions or socially functional practices: school exercises, elegies and epitaphs, commemorative volumes, complimentary verses, celebrations, entertainments, devotions, epistles.

Reading Milton's early poems one is aware of the poet not only adopting but in many cases actually performing particular social roles: it can even seem (almost) sensible to consider whether Milton really did attach *Sonnet VIII* ('Captain, or colonel, or knight in arms') to his door to disarm a potential Cavalier assault! As J. S. Smart noted in this case, 'we are in the presence of a poetical situation, not of a practical expedient',[27] but the distinction he makes is often far less applicable.

Underpinning any notion Milton may have had of 'the poetry simply as poetry'—in Eliot's phrase—is an active awareness of a range of practical uses of writing, of the various functions of particular writing practices as embodying and reinforcing Milton's relations to others as teacher, friend, correspondent, propagandist. Even when Milton formulates what might seem a purely 'aesthetic'

---

[26] *A Treatise of Civil Power in Ecclesiastical Causes*, preliminary address 'To the Parliament'. For convenience of reference I have quoted from John S. Diekhoff's invaluable volume, *Milton on Himself* (London, Cohen & West, 1965), p. 177, following his modernizations. Subsequent references will be to Diekhoff and to the Columbia Milton, *The Works of John Milton*, general editor Frank A. Patterson (New York, Columbia University Press, 1931-40), 20 volumes, abbreviated to *CM*.

[27] J. S. Smart, *The Sonnets of Milton* (Glasgow, Maclehose, Jackson, 1921), p. 57.

notion, the underlying Platonic conception indicates that the primary aim is fundamentally philosophical-theological, and even devotional, as in the letter to Diodati of 23 September 1637:

> What besides God has resolved concerning me I know not, but this at least: He has instilled into me, if into anyone, a vehement love of the beautiful. . . it is my habit day and night to seek for this Idea of the beautiful, as for a certain image of supreme beauty, through all the forms and faces of things (for many are the shapes of things divine) . . . [28]

When Henry Oldenburg suggested to Milton, in 1654, that his talents might be more worthily employed than in replying to the *Cry of the Royal Blood* Milton's response reveals rather different criteria from those Pattison, for example, would approve:

> To prepare myself, as you suggest, for other labours—whether nobler or more useful I know not, for what can be nobler or more useful in human affairs than the vindication of liberty?—truly . . I shall be induced to that easily enough . . not that in any way I repent of what I have done, since it was necessary; for I am far from thinking that I have spent my toil, as you seem to hint, on matters of inferior consequence. [29]

It is, indeed, in the prose writings concerned with 'the vindication of liberty', and not just in the poetry, that we find Milton appealing for or implying divine assistance and inspiration, and it has been plausibly suggested that Milton, by 1654, saw himself as having fulfilled his task of writing a national epic in, precisely, his authorship of the *Defensio*.[30] When any form of writing is recognized as performing a function over and essentially above any strictly 'literary'

---

[28] Diekhoff, p. 125, *CM*, XII, p. 27.
[29] Diekhoff, p. 136, *CM*, XII, p. 65.
[30] Cf. Diekhoff, pp. 222, 239.

satisfaction, the distinction between 'the prose' and 'the poetry' is far from primary.

Yet for a text to perform a particular social purpose effectively it must not only postulate but actually reach and influence its appropriate audience, and by August 1659 Milton is clearly unsure of his readership, as the opening paragraphs of *The Likeliest Means to Remove Hirelings* indicates:

> to whom should I address what I still publish . . but to you ['supreme Senate', Parliament] . . and to whom more appertain these considerations which I propound than to yourselves and the debate before you, though I trust of no difficulty, yet at present of great expectation, not whether ye will gratify (were it no more than so) but whether ye will hearken to the just petition of many thousands . . or whether ye will satisfy . . the covetous pretences and demands of insatiable hirelings

—and so, rather sadly, on.[31] By October 1659 Milton can only write a *Letter to a Friend concerning the Ruptures of the Commonwealth*—but the 'friend' was perhaps only a fiction, the *Letter* remained unpublished till 1698, and Milton himself admits to 'not finding that either God or the public required more of me than my prayers for them that govern'.[32] In the conclusion to the *Ready and Easy Way to Establish a Free Commonwealth*, of February 1660, as the 'restoration' loomed ever closer, Milton can barely pretend that he speaks to any actual audience, except, 'with the prophet', to the very stones—and to God Himself—and, perhaps, to the future.[33] The appeal to Urania, in the invocation to Book VII of *Paradise Lost*, must, by then, have seemed, if anything, over-optimistic:

> still govern thou my song,
> Urania, and fit audience find, though few.

[31] Diekhoff, p. 179, *CM*, VI, pp. 43f.
[32] Diekhoff, p. 183, *CM*, VI, p. 101.
[33] Diekhoff, p. 246, *CM*, VI, p. 148.

It is, or should be, a familiar argument that *Paradise Lost* can be read as Milton's theological attempt to make sense of the defeat of the 'good old cause' of God's own 'saints'. Since he had, to the very last, continued to believe in God's providential guidance of the political fate of the Revolution—even claiming the restoration of the Rump Parliament in May 1659 as 'a new dawning of God's miraculous providence among us' and calling upon God to 'suffer not' the final Restoration in *A Ready and Easy Way*[34] —Milton, when faced with the actual crushing fact of the Restoration, had somehow, still, to re-assert 'Eternal Providence' and 'justify the ways of God'—if only to himself.

To adapt Marx: Milton could now only attempt to understand, no longer to change, his world. But to do so involved not only speaking for God but also, in a sense, to God, as A. D. Nuttall has recently argued.[35] One might well suggest that Milton, in reciting the tale of mankind's fall and Christ's heroic redemption, finally assumes the traditional role of the epic poet, the court bard, he had once outlined in *Ad Patrem* (lines 41-49): he sings the exploits of his true and only king in the very presence of that king, a presence that takes the most intimate form of inspiration. But, in more mundane terms, the choice of the epic form, that anachronistic, timeless mode, indicates that Milton is no longer writing within or for any immediate social purpose or occasion: this poem is not a political intervention but a theological inquiry, albeit an inquiry into the very deepest roots of political possibility itself.

One can indeed interpret *Paradise Lost* as probing the most fundamental reasons of all for the defeat of God's 'saints', by associating that issue with the fiercely problematic nature of man's disobedience to God's will and with the desperately difficult question of the conditions for the final

---

34 Diekhoff, pp. 179, 246; *CM*, VI, pp. 43, 148.

35 A.D. Nuttall, *Overheard by God: Fiction and Prayer in Herbert, Milton, Dante and St John* (London, Methuen, 1980). Nuttall's acount of Herbert might be usefully compared with my own, in *Reading Relations*, (Harvester, 1982) [or *Literary Conversions*, 2015].

establishment of God's own kingdom. Yet such a cosmic extension of the immediate dilemma necessarily precludes any directly effective human rectification of the present political disaster. All that one could be required to do, as a post-Restoration reader of *Paradise Lost*, would be to acknowledge one's own participation in its overall scenario of Fall and Redemption—and reform oneself accordingly.

What is then interesting is how this absence of any immediately practical purpose or specific audience opens up the possibility of quite alternative ways of reading *Paradise Lost.* Not only Milton himself but, in various ways, all the opposing participants in the struggles of 1640-60 had sought for the intelligibility and justification of their political actions and fates in overtly theological categories. By the early eighteenth century this was no longer the case, for a variety of interlocking reasons which can only be cursorily noted here.

One central factor was a change in the relations and respective powers of what Althusser terms the 'ideological apparatuses'. An index to this basic shift would be that whereas in the 1630s the liaison between the Court and the Church endowed Archbishop Laud with decisive authority, by the reign of Queen Anne'it caused a sensation when, for the last time, a Bishop was appointed to government office'.[36] Another, related, facet of the change is that while the Civil War could certainly be seen by its participants as a conflict of large social and ideological forces, with divine intervention and interest claimed by all sides, for the generation which read the *Spectator* the crucial reference-point was 1688 not 1649 and both the constitutional settlement of 'the Glorious Revolution' and the subsequent jostlings and local manoeuvrings of 'Whigs' and 'Tories' seemed easily amenable to explanations far less grandiose, and far less noble, than the direct attentions of the Godhead.

More generally, one could claim that by the time Addison praised *Paradise Lost* the very notion of a seriously applied

---

36 Christopher Hill, *The Century of Revolution 1603-1714* (London, Sphere, 1969), p. 14.

theological explanation of the defeat of a political principle or party must have seemed extremely remote, and even quaint. An appeal might still be made, of course, to the benevolent oversight of the Deity upon British affairs ("God Save the King!") and the relevance of religious allegiance to the constitutional fate of James II was clear—but the change in ideological atmosphere has made theological explanations and vindications of political events seem increasingly redundant and perhaps even unintelligible in themselves. Indeed, something of that change is already apparent by the 1680s: when the preachers and pamphleteers of the 1640s characterized their opponents as 'sons of Belial' they intended a far more literal application[37] than, for example, Dryden did in writing, in 1681, of Lord Shaftesbury as 'Achitophel'.

If, however, by the 1700s the strictly theological dimension of *Paradise Lost* is no longer recognizable or even intelligible as a serious reaction to a specific political dilemma, the poem itself still required and prompted a response—and in Addison's treatment, above all, we can see taking shape not merely a reading of the poem 'as literature' but almost the very emergence of that notion of 'literature' itself which we have inherited. In broad terms, one could suggest that while Milton himself transposed his political dilemma into a theological form, Addison's essays transformed *Paradise Lost* from a theological inquiry into a (merely) 'literary' narrative, to be read primarily for its 'literary' qualities and secondarily, perhaps, as suitable devotional (not theological) matter for a Sunday.

This is not, of course, to say that *Paradise Lost* had not been responded to as a text with 'literary' qualities before Addison, but only that the eliding of any substantially theological or political significance of the poem in Addison's strictly 'literary' criticism encapsulates, concentrates and bequeaths to subsequent readers a notion of 'literature' (or Literature) as, precisely, defined by its distinction from 'non-literary' considerations which Milton would not himself have wholeheartedly endorsed. Addison's immensely influential

---

[37] Cf. Whiting, op. cit., Ch. VI.

essays on Milton did indeed become paradigmatic for the development of the allied notions of 'literature' and 'criticism' which underpin today's profession of 'literary criticism'.

It would take this essay too far afield to analyse Addison's role in that development in relation to his own political and ideological position[38] or to trace the full significance of his conception of 'literature' in the subsequent consolidation of an ideological notion of 'culture' in England, but a few concluding pointers can be given.

By the time of Macaulay's *Edinburgh Review* article on Milton, in August 1825—ostensibly a review of the recently discovered *De Doctrina*—the idea that Milton's own theology might be at all relevant to *Paradise Lost* can be casually acknowledged and perfunctorily disposed of in a sentence, while the lack of awareness of any substantial political dimension of the poem is apparent in Macaulay's use, for example, of a story from Ariosto concerning a 'foul' and 'loathsome' snake, without ever adverting to its resounding echoes of the problem of Satan's role in *Paradise Lost*.[39] For Macaulay, Milton's stature and reputation as a 'great poet' merely makes him extremely useful as a culturally prestigious ornament to claim for one's own party.

Some forty years later, Matthew Arnold's proposal that 'culture' and 'literature'—of which Milton is by then a supreme exemplar—might finally take the place of religious belief in our lives must seem the most perverse twist yet in

---

[38] Cf., for example, the interesting suggestions in L.A. Elioseff, 'Joseph Addison's Political Animal: Middle Class Idealism in Crisis', *Eighteenth Century Studies*, VI, no. 3 (Spring 1973), pp. 372-81. Dr. Leavis's doctorate was gained from writing about 18th c periodical criticism.

[39] Macaulay writes: 'Such a spirit is Liberty. At times she takes the form of a hateful reptile. She grovels, she hisses, she stings. But woe to those who in disgust shall venture to crush her! And happy are those who, having dared to receive her in her degraded and frightful shape, shall at length be rewarded by her in the time of her beauty and glory!' *Critical and Historical Essays* (London. Longmans, Green & Co., 1877), p. 19.

this history of the appropriation of Milton. But that honour, one can also claim, is reserved for Eliot and Leavis who, in effect, came close to treating *Paradise Lost* not as itself an attempt to understand the course of history in the seventeenth century but rather as itself part of the 'explanation' of what, for them, crucially 'happened' in that century. In the notion that 'a dissociation of sensibility set in'—the major evidence for which is Milton's work—we can see the extraordinary substitution of 'literary history' and 'cultural' explanation for both theological and political ways of making sense of history itself. For Eliot's own 'theology of history' we have to go, of course, to *Four Quartets*.

This over-compressed account only suggests an argument that would need to be elaborated at considerable length. Clearly, the overall development I have sketched is influenced by many other factors and is exceedingly complex, but the role of *Paradise Lost* as a central reference-point within that development can, I think, be connected back to its status as a theological response to a political situation. Once the text became dissociated from its context and its 'literary' qualities divorced from its political and theological dimensions it could be appropriated as simply devotional reading, literary 'classic', or harmless scholarly-critical fodder. Yet the text still carried its political and theological charge, most obviously in its treatment of Satan's rebellion, and those seriously concerned with either politics or theology, whether nineteenth-century Chartists or twentieth-century Christians and atheists, have, necessarily, recognized that to treat this poem 'simply as poetry' is to avoid its full challenge.

It seems appropriate that a generation of politically radical critics (in the wake of the 'defeat' of 1968?) have recently turned their attention to Milton.[40] It is clear, once

---

[40] See, for example, the essays on Milton by David Aers and Gunther Kress, Anthony Easthope, and Fredric Jameson, in *1642: Literature and Power in the Seventeenth Century, 'Proceedings of the Essex Conference on the Sociology of Literature'*, ed. Francis Barker *et al.* (University of Essex, 1981); Allen Grossman, 'Milton's Sonnet

again, that the 'civil war' is still being fought out over Milton, not least in the ideological battles over the very nature of 'literature' and 'criticism' at his own university.[41] With a nice sense of irony one marxist critic has even taken Eliot's and Leavis's criticisms of Milton and argued that the features they deplore are precisely those which a 'revolutionary criticism'derived from Benjamin and Derrida should exploit.[42]

An even deeper irony has, however, to be recognized in conclusion. It was a chaplain of King George IV who finally edited the *De Doctrina* in 1825, at His Majesty's command; in 1841 Prince Albert commissioned William Etty's *Comus* paintings for the garden pavilion of Buckingham Palace; and in 1981, at the wedding of the future King Charles III of England, it was a text by Milton that was sung while the happy couple signed the register.[43]

"On the Late Massacre in Piedmont": a note on the Vulnerability of Persons in a Revolutionary Situation', *Literature in Revolution*, ed. C. Newman and G.A. White (Boston, Holt, Rinehart and Winston, 1972), pp. 283-301; Michael Wilding, 'Regaining the Radical Milton', *The Radical Reader*, ed. S. Knight and M. Wilding (Sydney, Wild & Woolley, 1977), pp. 119-44; Robert Hodge, 'Satan and the Revolution of the Saints', *Literature & History*, No. 7 (Spring 1978), pp. 20-33; Andrew Milner, *John Milton and the English Revolution: a study in the sociology of literature* (London, Macmillan, 1981); and, of course, C. Hill, *Milton and the English Revolution* (London, Faber and Faber, 1977).

[41] Of those most prominently involved in recent [1982] disputes within the Cambridge English Faculty, Professor C. Ricks has written *Milton's Grand Style* and Dr Colin MacCabe is currently researching a book on Milton.

[42] Terry Eagleton, *Walter Benjamin or Towards a Revolutionary Criticism* (London, New Left Books, 1981), pp. 3-13.

[43] For Etty's paintings, see M.R. Pointon, *Milton and English Art* (Manchester University Press, 1970), pp. 208-12. The text sung at the Royal Wedding, 29 July 1981, was from Handel's *Samson*, 'Let the Bright Seraphim', adapted by Handel's librettist from Milton's 'At a Solemn Music', lines 10-13.

‘Simply as poetry’, as a purely aesthetic or merely devotional experience, Milton's work can still so easily be appropriated by those against whom he fought.

*

COLERIDGE : FRIEND OR PARTIZAN?[1]

> Unfortunately, in the great theatre of literature there are no authorized door-keepers: for our anonymous critics are self-elected. I shall not fear the charge of calumny if I add, that they have lost all credit with wise men, by unfair dealing: such as their refusal to receive an honest man's money (that is, his argument) because they anticipate and dislike his opinion, while others of suspicious character and most unseemly appearance, are suffered to pass without payment, or by virtue of orders which they have themselves distributed to known partizans. (I, 227).

Coleridge's comment on 'those, who under the name of Reviewers, volunteer this office', of the door-keepers of literature, seems to have passed unnoticed by many of his own reviewers. Of the reviews of *The Friend* I have seen, few have departed from the model drearily and anonymously exemplified in *The Times Literary Supplement*: a meticulous account, drawn almost entirely from Barbara Rooke's scholarly introduction, of the immediate circumstances in which *The Friend* was first published and later revised, a few (very well-deserved) compliments on the superb editing, and a final paragraph asserting the profundity and continuing worth of Coleridge's thought —and the job is done.

Such a response is doubly inappropriate in this case: because on Coleridge's own grounds the value of scholarship lies in the re-disclosure of the relevant in the dated, and because this particular work is concerned precisely with an attempt to outline underlying, 'fixed principles in politics, morals and religion' (title-page). To

[1] A review of *The Friend*, ed. B. E. Rooke, *Collected Works of Samuel Taylor Coleridge*, 4, RKP/Princeton University Press, 1969. Vol. I prints the 1818 *rifacimento*, Vol. II the original periodical of 1809-10, with various appendices. References are to Vol. I unless otherwise stated.

assert its continuing worth is to acknowledge both points; but, as Coleridge would agree, mere assertion is inadequate.

The assertion would not go unchallenged in any case: the possible relevance of even the recently dated, in whatever area, is under question today [1969-70], particularly, it is alleged, by that group loosely defined as 'the Underground'; if one seeks an alternative society, it is presumed, no compromise is allowed: the detritus of the previous is shovelled into the earth and buried, the radical eschewing even the roots that might grow from it. That the demand for such total cleavage exists is clear: it ranges from Rosenberg's *The Tradition of the New* through to a somewhat notorious article in *Slant* 20 which spoke of students as reduced to 'conscientious coprophagists' grubbily chewing the remnants of bourgeois culture, unnaturally subservient to 'reified knowledge'. The "We want it *NOW!!*" school collapses horizons in both directions—shedding even a revolutionary tradition demanding and embodying both historical diagnosis and future programme: analysis and strategy. It nevertheless—and this is part of the point of this article—remains a mark of that revolutionary tradition to understand and overcome the inadequacies of the inherited ideological modes which continue to sustain counter-revolutionary responses now.

Coleridge is one appropriate starting-point for such an analysis of the English "intellectual' tradition, viewed in the light of the marxist tradition which it so noticeably lacks. Coleridge wrote at a historical moment broadly characterized, in Europe as a whole, by the conjuncture of far-reaching changes in modes of production in Britain, and rapid changes in modes of social relation on the Continent, the former till recently often termed 'The Industrial Revolution', the latter stemming from 'the French Revolution'. But these 'revolutions', so often taken together as different aspects of the 'same' moment, were actually in one sense out of gear with each other.

Put very schematically and very crudely: England had already been through something akin to a bourgeois revolution (a premature Republic muted to a constitutional *modus vivendi* in 1688 which abandoned any 'mass' element emergent in the Civil War period), and was now, from 1780 onwards, entering a phase of technological advance which was the possible ground of a 'working-class' revolution, though this was in fact held and contained by the final bourgeois settlement of 1832—a Reform which rested on the reaction to an emergent but stifled revolutionary impetus from the barely-formed working-class. In France, the content of the Revolution, in an economic context increasingly post-feudal but some decades behind that of England, was in the end bourgeois (initially prompted in part, anyway, by the deep anglo-phile attitudes current among some French *philosophes*—an admiration precisely for the English bourgeois settlement); yet the form assumed by that revolution temporarily outstripped the contemporary English form by establishing a Republic rather than a constitutional monarchy; moreover the success of the French Revolution was partly ensured by the spectacular but short-lived role of the Parisian crowd, the 'masses'. The net result of this conjuncture of two different historical dislocations was a war between two empires, one basing itself on the military marshalling of the masses, the other on their proto-industrial recruitment to seriality—and the economic blockade imposed by the industrial power was, of course, decisive, finally curtailing any remnant possibilities of continental development beyond the bourgeois mode by the restoration of Louis XVIII as constitutional monarch in 1814.

Coleridge, publishing *The Friend* in 1809 and revising it in 1818, was—in these wider 'circumstances' far more important than the inadequacy of paper supplies at Penrith so lovingly treated by the *Times Literary Supplement* reviewer—not unnaturally confused in his reactions, only able, as a symptomatic example, to classify (along with many English contemporaries both within and without the 'movement") the emergent new revolutionaries of his own country as some kind of 'Jacobins'. This anxious response derived primarily from the (apparent) form of the French Revolution.

Only a short time after the Revolution, he had tried, in his earlier periodical *The Watchman* [2] of 1796—just two years after leaving Jesus College, Cambridge—both to keep to some extent journalistically abreast of current affairs and to provide original essays and commentary on political principles. That attempt was an uneasy one, in terms both of format and political position. Over half of its material was reprinted accounts of Parliamentary proceedings and extracts from other news-sources, the rest being composed of poems, letters, and essays, mainly by Coleridge but occasionally by various friends and some unsolicited contributors.

The response was predictable: provincial readers took it as a newspaper, to counter-balance the Government-controlled press which was almost the only source of news outside London (Flower's *Cambridge Intelligencer* and Montgomery's *Sheffield Iris* were lonely exceptions), while the London subscribers valued it for the essays. Unable fully to satisfy both, the journal folded after only ten issues. Politically, *The Watchman* began with explicit support, in the 'Prospectus', for the Whig Club's opposition to the Gagging Laws and for the Patriotic Societies' aim of general suffrage, but even by the first issue Coleridge had come to question both these positions. He actually gave some approval to the Gagging Acts as encouraging 'more cool and guarded' political discussion and perhaps leading to examination of 'first principles"; the question of suffrage was noticed finally in only one sentence of Number VI. The confused shifts in his specific reactions to the aftermath of the French Revolution can be traced even in the very short lifetime (1st March to 13th May, 1796) of the journal.

It was no surprise, then, that a decade later, in starting again a periodical of his own, Coleridge should have both aimed at a more definite audience and changed the format to exclude current news. By then he could see his only viable contribution as the attempt to spell out more single-mindedly 'first principles' that might be the basis of a

---

[2] Also usefully made available in the new *Collected Edition*, 2, *The Watchman*, ed. Lewis Patton, 1970.

political philosophy, not immediately tied to specific passing commentary and judgements.

Something of the same dilemma faces many political writers at present, particularly radicals, in an equally confused general situation.[3] One can curiously parallel the broad (and obviously crude) schematic analysis of Coleridge's historical moment above by a global sketch of our own period. Far-reaching shifts in both modes of production and modes of social relation again characterize the present, but again they are, at their most visible levels, separated out. The 'affluent' First World (U.S.A., Europe, Japan) faces acute problems arising from considerable technological advance (pollution, disposal of economic surplus, re-deployment, etc.), but the prospects, as distinct from the demands, for a radical overturning of social relations in the advanced West are hardly pressing. The Third World, however, is beginning to live through the tensions between modes (or effects) of a new technological level, well beyond the 'feudal' though still decades(?) 'behind' that of the West, and old forms of social organization that simply cannot co-exist with the new social relations engendered and necessitated by that technological level, and which increasingly give way before them. The Second World (U.S.S.R. and European Socialist Republics) is the ambivalent effect of a revolution which assumed the forms of a post-bourgeois world but in content resulted in its own mode of 'bourgeois' organization. And again an inter-imperial war, resting on military (albeit 'cold') and industrial dragooning on both sides, has dominated our historical consciousness. The early temptation of Western radicals of, say, the Thirties, to identify their programme with that of the Bolshevik Jacobins has obviously been surpassed. But the current temptation to identify with those

[3] For one symptomatic moment see the *Editorial* in the final issue of the Catholic-Marxist journal *Slant* (No. 30, March 1970)—a publication which also tried to hold in tension journalism and 'first principles' in a context of connections between 'politics, morals and religion'. Cf. also J. M. Cameron's criticism that the (first) English 'New Left' lacked a 'philosophy of man', *Night Battle*, pp. 50f.

areas where a successful leap-frogging of the bourgeois phase has perhaps been achieved (Cuba, China—after two revolutions in a generation, possibly Tanzania, soon perhaps Viet-Nam) ignores the fact that their historical economic-social dislocations are not ours: hence the fundamental irrelevance, to both analysis and strategy, of the Western Maoists at present. That our situation is complicated by the 'invisible earnings' relations between First, Second, and Third World and confused by the presence of pockets of the Third World grafted into the domestic exploitation in the First World ('immigration' and 'racial' problems) does not justify a simpliste game of putative leap-frog, forwards or backwards: we are in a bourgeois phase and we do not, presumably, advance beyond it by trying to go back to pre-industrial social relations and 'starting again', the thoughts of Chairman Mao in our fists (much as I might respect those thoughts for his situations). In other words, the radicals today who do seriously confront the problems of transition are, like Coleridge, driven back to basics—which includes their own thinking, critical reflection, not as a collapse into idealism but as an attempt to establish the dialectical bases of praxis.

Is there any possible value, then, in re-considering Coleridge's earlier grapplings with the same fundamental areas? His attempt, along with many 'Romantics', to think dialectically rather than discursively [4] (exemplified best in the movement and style, organization and tone, of the 1809 version) should itself be invitation enough, but I want in this article to focus primarily on the content of Coleridge's political thinking (as expressed rather in the 1818 *rifacimento*).

---

4. The distinction here is Jacobi's (whom Coleridge echoes frequently in *The Friend*), though linked to the more Marxist sense used above. Cf. also Coleridge's letter to Tom Poole, 25th January, 1810, justifying his use of parentheses: 'They are the drama of reason, and present the thought growing, instead of a mere *Hortus siccus.*'

The first point, therefore, to be clear about is the political position (on a narrower definition of politics) in which Coleridge stood at that stage. In 1795 he had approved of the revolutionary ideals of the French and opposed any British military counter-action. In 1809 he had supported the war against Napoleon and was vigorously denying the charges that he had once been a 'Jacobin', equating Jacobinism moreover with 'democracy and sedition' (II, 105). By 1818 he was firmly against the moves at home towards electoral reform, on the grounds that education must precede political change.

The Friend was begun as a contribution to that 'education', but its sights were clearly élitist (the subscribers numbered 400-600) and the general position idealist. A typical passage in 1809 (No. 4, II; 52) exemplifies both assumptions: he asserts that all national histories are 'accounts of noble structures raised by the wisdom of the few, and gradually undermined by the ignorance and profligacy of the many . . the deficiency of good, which everywhere surrounds us, originates in the general unfitness and aversion of men to the process of thought, that is to continuous reasoning. '

This emphasis on the role of ideas, located in an elite, prompts Coleridge to preface his major sections on principles in politics, etc., by an examination of the conditions necessary for the 'com-munication of truth' (Essays i to xvi). He considers in this section such topics as the freedom of the press, tolerance, the laws of libel, censorship, etc., and makes some interesting points—distinguishing verbal accuracy from veracity (42, 49), arguing for a recognition that 'man may be made better, not only in consequence, but by the mode and in the process, of instruction' (103).

However, the limits on his analysis are clear throughout: even this last comment is made in a context of wishing that 'a hundred men' would acknowledge this insight. The freedom of communication he seeks is in the final analysis administrative: presuming that communication of a dialogue kind will be restricted to the already 'educated' elite, he demands the removal of restrictions on their power to publish. But the hedges round this position are high: 'free inquiry of the boldest kind' is, of course, allowable—provided 'that it is evidently intended for the perusal of those only, who may be presumed to be capable of weighing the arguments' (42; presumed by whom?).

Though, in contrast, he later wants to maintain that in criticism of governments 'the facts are commonly as well known to the readers as to the writer', yet any criticism which might lead to the 'subversion of government and property' or which might help to 'render the lower classes turbulent and apt to be alienated from the government of their country' (isn't that the issue ?) is obviously to be ruled out of court—though again at this point Coleridge is even prepared to argue against his general idealist position, with a remark on 'the very great improbability that such effects will be produced by such writings', and even to argue that 'the frequency of open political discussion . . indisposes a nation to overt acts of sedition and conspiracy. " They talk ill", said Charles the Fifth, "of the Belgian provinces, but they suffer so much the better for it." ' (93).

These two main limits—restriction to an elite and an ambivalent attitude to the power of revolutionary writing—are caught in his comment on Luther: 'in his circular letter to the Princes, on occasion of the Peasants' War, he uses a language so inflammatory, and holds forth a doctrine which borders so near on the holy right of insurrection, that it may well remain untranslated' (139).

The liberal contradictions that Coleridge clearly exemplifies here force him simultaneously to argue for the freedom of the press and yet to provide grounds for the actual gagging of the press in his own day—the specific results of which, following his option against providing 'news', he never mentions. In 1810, for example, Cobbett was fined £1,000 and imprisoned for two years for protesting against military flogging. In 1812 Eaton was pilloried and given eighteen months' imprisonment for publishing Paine's *Age of Reason.* In 1817 Sidmouth authorized commitment by a magistrate of anyone even *suspected* of 'libel'. Though Coleridge exulted in Hone's acquittal for blasphemous libel, on political libels he remains fixed in the liberal presumptions that everything can be changed by discussion kept within the limits of the law, while also excluding from discussion the majority of people: plead *for* the oppressed not *to* them, teach the poor rather their duties initially, using the Gospel to 'ensure obedience' (374-5; this passage is from 1795). Moreover, one must not allow 'unnatural influences' to enter a political discussion—such as 'bitter declamations against the follies and oppression of the higher classes' or 'details of present calamity or immediate suffering, fitted to excite the fury of the multitude'. The limits of this kind of liberalism recur again and again in the English tradition: half a century after the original publication of *The Friend*, Mill continues to argue:

> An opinion that corn-dealers are starvers of the poor, or that private property is robbery, ought to be unmolested when simply circulated through the press, but may justly incur punishment when delivered orally to an excited mob assembled before the house of a corn-dealer, or when handed about among the same mob in the form of a placard. (*On Liberty*, 1859, ch. III).

The liberal is quite prepared for 'free speech' provided it remains in fact free of any concrete engagement with the structural realities of oppression. A century after Mill, the Underground press is 'free' (production costs are cheaper, but TV is now dominant, and the print market is capitalist anyway)—until it achieves a wide enough circulation actually to bite: hence the recent raids on *Black Dwarf* and the technical prosecution of *IT*—the only Underground papers in England to break beyond the strangle of distribution. The recent pronouncements of *The Times Literary Supplement* (25/12/69) dismissing the 'Underground press' are part of the same tradition, and have been appropriately demolished (in beautiful pseudo-*TLS* style) by Sanford Berman's letter (22/1/70) documenting endless persecution in the States and England.

One could develop the analysis of the role of communications in terms of the current debate among the Left on the primacy or subordination of cultural studies, and about the kind of communications-analysis appropriate.[5] We will return to the roots of this problem later, in indirect fashion, but Coleridge's inconsistencies on this topic need first to be tracked to their source.

That source is clearly revealed in the 'Section the First on the Principles of Political Knowledge' (163-338). To summarize broadly, Coleridge here applies the psychological categories of *Sense*, *Understanding,* and *Reason* to characterize different political philosophies and options. His dismissal of the 'Sense'-based system (of Hobbes) is brief and aspects of the argument will hardly convince the present generation, though they may share his judgements:

> A vast Empire may perhaps be governed by fear; at least the idea is not absolutely inconceivable, under circumstances which prevent the consciousness of a common strength . . but a million of insulated individuals is only an abstraction of the mind . . the whole Theory is baseless. We are told by History, we learn from our experience, we know from our own hearts, that fear, of itself, is utterly incapable of producing any regular, continuous and calculable effect, even on an individual; and that the fear which does act systematically upon the mind, always presupposes a sense of duty, as its cause. (167)

A generation whose 'History' is told in terms of Hitler, Stalinism, Apartheid, 'brain-washing', *The Lonely Crowd* and *The Authoritarian Personality*, will not so easily accept Coleridge's distinction between fear and choice dictated by duty, as the substratum of social cohesion. Nor will it be entirely bemused by Coleridge's option for a political mode

---

[5] I have discussed some overall problems of the contemporary communications media for radicals in 'Sit down snd be counted', *Slant* 29, January 1970.

resting on the pragmatic'Expediency' of Understanding (177). Wilsonism is too close to us for that.

Rather, the fascination still present in Coleridge's analysis here (essays iii and iv, 176-202) lies in his account of the inadequacies of *Reason* as a basis of politics, upon which he firmly rests his preference for *Understanding*. Though Coleridge admits that

> . . from Reason alone can we derive the principles which our Understandings are to apply, the Ideal to which by means of our Understandings we should endeavour to approximate (199)

he wants to maintain that 'Human institutions cannot be wholly constructed on principles of Science, which is proper to immutable objects' (176).[6] He argues for this conclusion mainly by attacking Rousseau and through him Paine's writings (a few years later and he would have had to attack Bentham's now neglected pamphlets).

Coleridge summarizes Rousseau as saying that the only constitution which is legitimate is that which is 'capable of being demonstrated out of the original laws of the pure Reason' (cf. 178). The argument underlying Rousseau's system, he alleges, is roughly as follows. All voluntary actions are moral, but all morality is grounded in Reason. Every man is born with Reason, and without it would be a thing not a person. The distinction between person and thing (end and means) is the ground of all law, which recognizes a man as a free agent, unable to disown his legal and moral responsibility as person. This equality before the law rests on the recognition that in respect of their Reason all men are equal. Since society is an aggregate of individuals, society cannot impose notions of Right and Wrong on any man, except those 'contained in the common Reason. ' Rousseau's perfect constitution, then, is one in which each man 'uniting with the whole, shall yet obey himself only and

6 Motto to essay iii, from Robert South; this first sentence is, interestingly, not in South, but probably Coleridge's own addition.

remain as free as before': in obeying laws based on Reason the man of Reason obeys himself. A society can only arrive at this happy state by allowing all the individuals to decide the common law. In the process, any prejudices will cancel themselves out. (cf. 190-193.)

Clearly, as Coleridge points out, this argument collapses at the last stage: prejudices may reinforce one another, leading to a common error. From this flaw, Coleridge can argue that Rousseau's system leads both to Napoleon and to the *laissez-faire* politics of individualism. The only alternative, then, is a system of politics based not on Reason, but on Understanding. Significantly, however, Coleridge, in order to summarize the final stage of that argument, uses a quotation not from Rousseau but from Burke.

For in fact Coleridge has ignored two crucial premisses and conditions of Rousseau's position: 'if the People, engaged in deliberation, were adequately informed' and, secondly, if there were no over-dominant groups influencing public opinion in the society (cf. *du Contrat Social*, ch. 3). Coleridge had, in fact, already ignored this step in his earlier 'refutation' of Rousseau's position, that all men are equal in respect of their Reason:

> . . though the Reason itself is the same in all men, yet the means of exercising it, and the materials (i.e. the facts and ideas) on which it is exercised, being possessed in very different degrees by different persons, the practical Result is, of course, equally different — and the whole ground of Rousseau's Philosophy ends in a mere Nothingism' (159).

Rousseau's point, however, is, precisely, to make available to all men the necessary ''facts and ideas' (rejecting, incidentally, the very notion of 'possession' in this area) and to equalize the 'means of exercising' Reason. The debate is still with us, of course, though now in terms of the validity of I.Q. testing and the proposals of the Black Paper.

One could analyse further Coleridge's various misunderstandings of Rousseau (especially of *Volonté de tous* and *Volonté generale*) or examine Rousseau's actual contributions to current radical thought.[7] But what is particularly interesting in Coleridge's failure to summarize Rousseau fairly is that the premise he omits is precisely the condition on which Coleridge himself had first focussed his attention in *The Friend* : the adequacy of 'the predominant state of public opinion' (181), an adequacy which depends on the absence of any power with disproportionate control over the public media.

Once again, it is the ambivalence of Coleridge's attitude to the revolutionary potential of mass information and public opinion that clearly underlies his 'misunderstanding'. His basic option for Expediency, in other words, does not in fact rest on an argument that holds, but rather on a deep prejudice that presumes. How much it presumes must be examined next, but it is worth remarking at this point that the notion of 'Reason' has, from very different considerations, become suspect also to the present generation seeking an alternative society based on the fusion of individual and social decision. For 'Reason' has been a difficult term to sustain in the twentieth century. Max Horkheimer's *Eclipse of Reason* sketchily treats some aspects of its demise, and others have been revealed in the subordination of (academic) rationality to political ideologies—a process analysed again and again from Orwell's seminal essays to Chomsky's *American Power and the New Mandarins*. But the basic reason (pardon the word) surely lies in the rise since, precisely, Hegel's response to the French Revolution, of that area of interest which now constitutes 'sociology of consciousness'—again notably absent, as a discipline or approach, from an English academic tradition that escaped the rise of continental sociology in general.[8]

---

[7] Cf. e.g. G. Della Volpe, *Rousseau e Marx* and 'The marxist critique of Rousseau', *New Left Review* 59; L. Althusser, 'Sur le Contrat Social (les Décalages)', *Les Cahiers pour l'Analyse*, 8.

[8] Cf. Herbert. Marcuse, *Reason and Revolution*; P. Berger and T. Luckmann, *The Social Construction of Reality*; Perry Anderson, 'Components of the National Culture', *Student Power* (Penguin), J-P. Sartre, *Critique de la Raison Dialectique*.

The second part of this essay will return to the problem of the relation between modes of rationality and social group, but for the moment we can note that no matter how great the present difficulty of the notion of reason, that can hardly excuse those 'revolutionaries' who are apparently content, to use Coleridge's harsh shaft, 'to live as alms-folks on the opinions of their contemporaries and . . reconcile themselves to the *sans-culotterie* of their ignorance by scoffing at the useless fox-brush of Pedantry' (212)— beware Fontana Masters!

*

The contention that Coleridge's rejection of Rousseau's 'Reason' as a political principle is based on a deep-seated prejudice can be clearly established if we analyse further the roots of his own political position. Just as his plea for more adequate communication of truth is ultimately a petition for administrative reform, the nature of 'truth' itself being analysed at this stage only in terms of the difference between what is self-evident and what must be demonstrated (55f), so his definition of politics is ultimately a reduction to 'administration', to how things 'ought to be managed' (214). That this conveniently forgets that politics is also about policies, i.e. about morality—a position that Coleridge will otherwise argue for—is clear from the use of the term 'political' in his criticism of Cartwright: that he

> confounds the sufficiency of the conscience to make every person a moral and amenable Being, with the sufficiency of judgment and experience requisite to the exercise of political Right (207).

This position has its epistemological roots in his distinction between the 'truths' of science and the 'probability' of facts of experience (158)—a distinction which holds politically, provided one genuinely acknowledges the equal validity of quite different 'experience'.

The practical outcome of Coleridge's position is a politics which can meet an argument that the expenditure on one naval operation to destroy nine French ships could have provided instead £100 for 2,000 poor families or built a new town in every English county, by the response: 'These men know that it is not practicable' (244).

An age which could award its admirals £20 for every enemy corpse— more than the average annual wage of its own living labourers—or, in our own age, a country which can spend $904 billion on military power and $96 billion on education, health, welfare housing and community development (Chomsky, *op. cit.*, p. 106) has need of such responses. At least in the extreme example of a country signing away its national independence, Coleridge can admit that it is the people not the 'half-dozen individuals possessing the government of those countries' that must choose, morally and politically:

> . . is it to be supposed for a moment, that a whole nation, consisting of perhaps twenty millions of human souls, could ever have invested a few individuals, whom, altogether for the promotion of its welfare it had entrusted with its government, with the right of signing away its existence ? (275).

In a world mapped out by the putative trajectories of inter-continental nuclear missiles, those words now have a far grimmer edge—one that bit deep into the consciousness of a rebel generation which first expressed itself in CND.

For what this mode of politics has always deeply presumed is that—generalizing Coleridge's account of his era as coming after all major changes— 'to us there remain only quiet duties, the constant care, the gradual improvement, the cautious unhazardous labours of the industrious though contented gardener' (168). For the liberal, ours is always a post-revolutionary age—and he will, if necessary, regretfully endorse considerable violence to keep it that way. His own direct contribution tends to be interpretative: to explain away the revolutionary needs and movements of his own age.

Coleridge, of course, attempts to do just this, by desperately differentiating the 'privations, sufferings, and manifold oppressions of the great mass of the Continental population', 'the unutterable abominations of their oppressors', and their 'disgusting forms of despotism', from 'the real blessings of English law' and 'the executive branch of the English sovereignity' (cf. 214-216). True, he declares, in France "there was indeed a general disposition to change and rebellion', but in England

> there was not a city, not a town, in which a man suspected of holding democratic principles could move abroad without receiving some unpleasant proof of the hatred in which his supposed opinions were held by the great majority of the people. (218-219)

A period which could see the radical London Corresponding Society grow from nine members to 2,000 in a fortnight (1792), or the Society for Constitutional Information organize a street masquerade of 6,000 to celebrate the *sans-culotte* victory at Valmy (1792), or one town, Sheffield, collect 10,000 signatures challenging the House of Lords' existence (1793), and during which Paine's *Rights of Man: Pt. I* sold 50,000 copies in 1791 and *Pt. II* 200,000 in 1793 (in a population of 10 million which bought only 30,000 copies of Burke's *Reflections*[9]—such a period could hardly be described as Coleridge wanted it to be by 1809, and as many later historians still would like it to be. They too would echo Coleridge's impeccable liberal accents in his ostensibly sane and balanced reaction:

> The most prudent, as well as the most honest mode of defending the existing arrangements, would have been, to have candidly admitted what could not in truth be denied, then to have shewn that, though the things complained of were evils, they were necessary evils; or if they were removeable, yet that the consequences of the heroic medicines recommended by the Revolutionaries would be far more dreadful than the disease. (215)

---

[9] Cf. Gwyn Williams, *Artisans and Sans-Culottes*; E. P. Thompson, *The Making of the English Working Class.*

It was, however, the 'existing arrangements' that most deeply linked France and England. Whatever the differences, in both countries there existed a minority in control of a majority, that control resting ultimately on the control of property. Though Coleridge deprecated the 'panic of property' and questioned the grounds on which the inherited right to that property was defended by the ultra-right Anti-Jacobins, that he too defended property was never in doubt.[10] He opens Essay vi with the statement:

> From my earliest manhood, it was an axiom in Politics with me, that in every country where property prevailed, property must be the grand basis of government; and that that government was the best, in which the power or political influence of the individual was in proportion to his property

—adding, of course, the characteristically liberal and politically meaningless condition, 'provided that the free circulation of property was not impeded by any positive laws or customs'. (223)

This position he had already justified to his own satisfaction in his earlier debate with Rousseau and Cartwright. Against Rousseau, he declares: 'The chief object for which men first formed themselves into a State was not the protection of their lives but of their property. . But where individual landed property exists, there must be inequality of property'—for men are unequal, and one must respect their inequality (a respect shared by Marx, Lenin and Rousseau; what they further demanded was that men should also respect those less equal than themselves). Against Cartwright he argues that if, as Cartwright asserted, 'Laws to bind all must be assented to by all, and consequently every man, even the poorest, has an equal right to suffrage . . (because) . . all without exception are capable of feeling happiness or misery, according as they are well or ill

[10] At least in *The Friend*. Coleridge's Notebooks of this period are less positive.

governed', since, adds Coleridge, happiness or misery also depends on possessing the means of a comfortable subsistence, 'might not then, on the same or equivalent principles a Leveller construct a right to equal property?' Since universal suffrage in fact would give a legal power of abolishing or equalizing property, Coleridge feels quite content to 'answer' Cartwright by quoting back at him one of Cartwright's own 'Principles': 'That a power which ought never to be used ought never to exist' (199-202). For Coleridge the idea of abolishing property was as morally unthinkable as the idea of nuclear retaliation should be for any Christian now: the very threat 'ought never to exist'.

That Coleridge found the abolition or equalization of property almost un-thinkable drives us deeper, to perhaps the core of his political attitudes: his presumption that the Law is legitimate.[11] He clearly sees a connection between property and law: 'o property . . and to its inequalities, all human laws directly or indirectly relate' (200). But the relationship implied here is obscured by its mystified reversal. Using an anecdote about Alexander Ball's liberal handling of naval discipline, Coleridge sings:

> An invisible power it was, that quelled them, a power which was therefore irresistible, because it took away the very will of resisting. It was the aweful power of LAW acting on natures pre-configured to its influences. . . Who dares struggle with an invisible combatant? with an enemy which exists and makes us know its existence— but where it is, we ask in vain— No space contains it—

[11] Since I have accused Coleridge throughout of 'prejudice', perhaps I should remark here that pre-judice means taking the law for granted. Cf. also privi-lege. Note too that the fallacy of the notion of 'negative liberty' so strong in the liberal tradition (cf. 'no positive laws' above) lies in its forgetting that present law is the legitimization of the end-term of a previous historical process which it takes for granted as legitimate. Coleridge's attitudes to law are more complex than this (cf. his argument against the 'Antiquarians', and his *Addresses on Sir Robert Peel's Bill*, 1818) but not, in the result, radically different.

> time promises no control over it—it has no ear for any threats—it has no substance, that my hands can grasp or my weapons find vulnerable—it commands and cannot be commanded—it acts and is insusceptible of my reaction—the more I strive to subdue it, the more am I compelled to think of it—and the more I think of it, the more do I find it to possess a reality out of my-self, and not to be a phantom of my own imagination. (171)

In their own different styles, Dickens, Marx and Kafka could all re-write this passage—but hardly its continuation:

> . . that all, but the most abandoned men, acknowledge its authority, and that the whole strength and majesty of my country are pledged to support it; and yet that *for me* its power is the same with that of my own permanent Self, and that all the choice which is permitted to me, consists in having it for my Guardian Angel or my avenging Fiend! This is the Spirit of LAW! . . This is the true necessity, which compels man into the social state, now and always, by a still-beginning, never-ceasing force of moral cohesion. (171)

The mundane fact that English laws derived finally from a Commons composed largely of undistinguished younger sons and place-men seems momentarily to have escaped Coleridge.

This mystification is not, however, only Coleridge's. As he rightly points out (though he sees it as differentiating France and England), this sense of The Law as primary and alienated from specific human creation, has also entered deep into the consciousness of those whom it most affects:

> . . in Great Britain, a tyrant, who has abused [*sic*] the power, which a vast property has given him, to oppress a whole neighbourhood, can walk in safety unarmed and unattended, amid a hundred men, each of whom feels his heart burn with rage and indignation at the sight of him. . To what does the oppressor owe his safety ? To the spirit quelling thought: the laws of God and my country have

made his life sacred! I dare not touch a hair of his head! (168)

Law, like the invisible earnings which entwine the exploited abroad, is a silent, clean and highly effective weapon: the conscience as castration. (It is surely appropriate that it is through Fleet Street and past St Paul's that one travels from Chancery Lane to reach the Stock Exchange; the other way is via Newgate.) The Law becomes, in Coleridge's thought, the unquestioned arbiter even of sanity, of reason: 'What man in his senses would regard the faithful observation of a contract entered into to plunder a neighbour's house, but as a treble crime? ' (173)—but there are different possible definitions of sanity, crime, contract, plunder—and even neighbour. To re-define those terms would redefine our society, but to do so means first seeing the law in a different light.

Coleridge anxiously recognized this possibility—hence his attacks on that ultimate re-definition: the Code Napoleon (cf. 87-88, 173, 184, 198, etc.). Further, for Coleridge, the 'destruction of the Athenian constitution by the ascendancy of its democratic element' was brought about in part by the Sophists' extension of access to learning beyond the élite and by the attack on religion, and finally by 'the frequency of perjury' (438-442). Coleridge gives an interesting account, using Plato's character Callicles in the *Georgias*, of the argument behind this refusal to acknowledge the validity of Athenian Law: that 'aws, honour and ignominy were all calculated for the advantage of the law-makers' and that the Sophists saw those law-makers as protecting themselves from those stronger than themselves by legally enshrining the doctrine of equality (443).

What is almost laughable is that Coleridge equates the Sophists with the Jacobins—whose doctrine of equality he had earlier expended great energy combating. As in Coleridge's treatment of Rousseau, this case of 'muddled' thinking has its clear ideological undertow. For one can cut through Coleridge's mystificatory, topsy-turvy notion of law as that on which property is dependent, by a comment from a man whom he called a 'former Jacobin' (180)—Cromwell—but quoted by a Lord Chancellor who, more than any other man in the nineteenth century, grappled with and constantly reformed English laws: Henry Brougham:

> But (said Cromwell) the sons of Zeraiah are too strong for us, and we cannot mention the reformatting of the law but they presently cry out we design to destroy property, whereas the law, as it is now constituted, serves only to maintain the lawyers, and to encourage the rich to oppress the poor. (Brougham, *Memoirs*, 1871, III, 440).

It is perhaps mildly hopeful that as this review is being written the two cases in the headlines are, in England, the invasion of the High Court by Welsh Nationalists who received sentences of three months' imprisonment for 'contempt of court' and, in the USA (land of 'Law and Order'), the pre-trial hearings of the Black Panthers, which was described by a contemporary liberal journalist, Alistair Cooke in the *Guardian* (6.2.70), as one continuous contempt of court—though despite constant scuffles and interruptions the first person actually to be committed for contempt of court was a woman who asked: "And who judges the judge?" Precisely. Alistair Cooke finished his account by commenting that once respect for law and obedience to the courts has gone 'the whole game of democracy is up' That the very term 'democracy' can now appear in a liberal context 150 years after Coleridge, might even indicate that the word will one day cease to refer to a game.

This essay has already suggested at times that a more adequate 'epistemological' starting-point for a political philosophy would be somewhere in the area of sociology of consciousness—particularly that of class-consciousness. This is not the place to explore this problem in detail, but only to point a direction.[12] For both Coleridge and many of

---

12 Cf. e.g. S. Ossowski, *Class Structure in the Social Consciousness*; another Polish thinker is also important in this debate, cf. my review of L. Kolakowski, *Marxism and Beyond*, *New Blackfriars*,

the present generation 'Reason' is indeed an unhelpful notion,[13] but their different reasons for querying it lead into very different political arguments. While Coleridge maintains that life cannot reflect the exactness of Reason, the tendency now is to see specific forms of rationality as themselves reflections of specific forms of life—as rationalizations. In both cases something akin to a political pragmatism is the logical next step. The crucial difference lies in the recognition by the present generation of radicals that the basic political conflict is not one primarily of ideas, which liberal discussion might dissolve, but one of forms of life, their opposition (the concrete contradictions of the world, not contra-dictions between propositions) sustained by property relations and justified by those ideological language-games which are taken-for-granted from within particular forms of life. This is presumably familiar.

What is however interesting is that Coleridge himself at times recognized the deep inter-penetration of ideology and experience, not just in the case of law cited earlier ('acting on natures pre-configured to its influences') but also more widely: he remarks that "in an age in which artificial knowledge is received almost at birth, intellect and thought alone can be our upholder and judge' (124). But though even 'the meanest of men has his Theory, and to think at all is to theorize' (189), Coleridge recognizes that much that passes for thinking is merely an intensification of inherited 'artificial knowledge".

Some years after *The Friend*, Coleridge clarified his political position on the relation between property and intellect: in *On the Idea of the Constitution of Church and State* (1829) Coleridge argues first the need for a national 'Clerisy'—educators resident in every village and town, concerned with 'cultivating . . the harmonious development of those qualities and faculties that characterize our

---

September, 1969. [See also my *Autobiography & Class Consciousness*, forthcoming.]

13 The notion of "rights and duties', linked to it, also seem inadequate to many at present; cf.della Volpe, *op. cit.*—and Brecht's play, *The Caucasian Chalk Circle.*

humanity'. But he also argues that an intelligentsia without property and/or unmarried (marriage for Coleridge was 'the simplest . . form of property', 200) should have no political power.

In this conjunction of two attitudes to intellectuals we have the authentic voice of a later tradition, simultaneously 'intellectual' and anti-intellectual, ultimately concerned (to use Coleridge's description of his Clerisy's function) "to train the people of the country to be obedient, useful and organizable subjects, citizens and patriots, living to the benefit of the State and prepared to die for its defence'. There might be distinctions made within the 'people' and various substitutes might now be offered for 'the State', but the pre-sumptions remain.

In the wider perspective which I have tried briefly to indicate throughout, phrases from the quotation at the beginning of this article begin to echo with a more sinister ring: 'anonymous . . self-elected', 'I shall not fear the charge of calumny if I add that they have lost all credit', 'they anticipate and dislike his opinion', 'while others . . are suffered to pass without payment . . by virtue of orders which they themselves distributed to known partizans. ' The clash between partisans of different sides in intellectual matters, in 'the great theatre of literature', cannot be disentangled, as we have seen in Coleridge's case, from deep-seated political attitudes, our roots in our own limited forms of life and experience. The presence now, in England and America, of what may soon almost merit the name of an 'Anti-Clerisy', composed of a wide scattering of counter-educators who have endeavoured to redefine existentially the nature both of property and of marriage, as a prelude to releasing them for an active redefinition of society, has disclosed again the connections between art and politics: on the one side, the Arts Labs, the Anti-Universities, the poetry readings, guerrilla theatre, Underground press and films, the committed music groups, the opposition journals directly concerned with arts-politics, all linked to new senses of living; on the other—as the cartoon said—"It's nice to see the police so interested in Culture these days."

*

Obviously, this essay, too, is partisan. But it is not only lingering liberal-at-heart symptoms or sympathies that persuade me to end on a note of approval. The essays on 'the Principles of Method' (448-524), originally intended as an introduction to an encyclopaedia, are far from the only essays worth careful, probing encounter in these volumes: the whole periodical takes us close to the core of Coleridge; but these essays closest. I can only briefly indicate the depth of some of the shafts opened here: the first essay in the section begins with a few pages (448ff.) that anticipate aspects of Basil Bernstein's work, of Heidegger, and of Merleau-Ponty; from then on the reverberations are endless, touching major contributions in many disciplines that have become only recently living elements in our sense of ourselves. The pre-echoes range from T. S. Kuhn on paradigmatic shifts through Max Black on scientific metaphors and Charles Hartshorne on wonder, to the early developments of existentialism (Coleridge is the second writer in English to use 'existential' in a modern sense), while the very problematic of the essay itself looks back to Descartes' *Discours de la Méthode* and forward to Sartre's *Questions de Méthode*. For theologically-oriented readers, the anticipation of Dewart's recent contention against Sartre (the choice of the incomprehensible rather than the absurd) might save them 500 pages of *Foundations of Belief*; but they would do even better—bearing in mind the connections between Coleridge and Newman on development and Lonergan on method—to allow Coleridge's conception of method itself to sink deep: 'All Method supposes a principle of unity with progression; in other words, progressive transition without breach of continuity' (476)—there are partisans too in all theologies.

Finally, may I add to the general admiration for the exact academic training that reveals itself in the editing of these volumes, a word of awed admiration for the anonymous working printers who also produced this edition: in a total of some 1,800 pages there are probably no more than two or three printing errors. It is on such work also, in various ways, that serious scholarship depends.

*

NEWS FROM NOWHERE:
detail and desire

> To anyone not deeply interested in the social question it could not be at all an attractive book. It is true that it is cast in the form of a romance, but the author states very frankly in his preface that he has only given it this form as a sugar-coating to the pill, and the device of making a man wake up in a new world has grown so common, and has been done with so much more care and art . . that by itself this would have done little for it; it is the serious essay and not the slight envelope of romance which people have found interesting to them.

A literary critic today might well find this an apposite judgement on William Morris's *News from Nowhere*. The book has certainly attracted attention as a 'serious essay', as an almost unique instance of the Utopian imagination at work within the marxist tradition of social critique,[1] but for readers and critics attuned to the assumptions and conventions of nineteenth-century literary realism the work clearly offers a thin experience: one could easily articulate their predictable unease at the lack of complex characterisation, the absence of any delicate exploration of moral sensibility, the paucity of densely felt life.[2]

Yet it is precisely in its oblique relation to the more central instances of 'the Victorian novel' that *News* provokes critical consideration. Our very puzzlement as to whether to read it as 'a novel' at all might alert us to some of the limits of current critical conceptions of 'the novel'. What one can

---

[1] Cf. E. P. Thompson, *William Morris: Romantic to Revolutionary* (London, 1955) and Paul Meier, *William Morris: the Marxist dreamer* (Hassocks, 1978). The *Postscript* to the second edition of Thompson's book (London, 1977) surveys work on Morris in the last twenty years. *News from Nowhere* was first published serially in 1890, in *Commonweal*, the paper of the Socialist League.

[2] Cf. the useful comments in the Introduction to *News from Nowhere*, ed. J. Redmond (London. 1970), pp. xxiv-xxv. Redmond, however, seems to deny the appropriateness of any 'literary criticism' to *News*.

loosely term a Jamesian approach to fiction,[3] can be contrasted with, and even supplemented by, a 'sociology of literature' which concentrates on ''popular fiction', yet there are some nineteenth-century works which seem unamenable to bracketing either with George Eliot, Dickens and Thackeray in an extended great tradition or with G. W. M. Reynolds, G. P. R. James, Mrs Marsh and the cheap fiction of the Parlour or Railway Library.

News from Nowhere, like perhaps Peacock's conversation novels, Butler's *Erewhon* and Mallock's *The New Republic*, seems to straddle and implicitly challenge our current critical categories and methods. That *News* did once enjoy a steady popularity, at least among politically conscious workers, can be accounted for largely in terms of its explicit content,[4] but now, with a re-awakening of interest in the political or ideological significance of literary form,[5] it is perhaps the relation of *News* to the formal procedures of Victorian fiction that might win it a certain critical place; its very oddness as a 'novel' might prove illuminating.

News itself includes a number of comments about Victorian fiction which indicate Morris's own awareness of standing askew to a dominant tradition. In the second chapter Dick says of Boffin, the dustman whose name recalls Dickens, that:

---

[3] 'Jamesian' is perhaps the most appropriate term in this context, bearing in mind the relevance, for the critical issues raised by the propagandist intention of *News*, of the exchanges between James and H. G. Wells about the purposes and function of fiction; cf. *Henry James to H. G. Wells*, ed. L. Edel and G. N. Ray (London, 1958), especially James's letter of 10 July 1915, pp. 265-68.

[4] In the 1930s, Harold Laski found copies of *News* 'in home after home of the miners', even when most of the furniture had been sold; cf. Paul Thompson, *The Work of William Morris* (revised edition, London, 1977), p. 239. For some rather caustic comments on the influence of Morris's 'dream of socialism' on some Glasgow socialists, cf. Harry McShane, *No Mean Fighter* (London, 1978), pp. 30,33.

[5] Cf. e.g. Terry Eagleton, *Criticism and Ideology* (London, 1976), especially Chapter 4.

> he has a weakness: he will spend his time in writing reactionary novels, and is very proud of getting the local colour right, as he calls it; and as he thinks that you come from some forgotten comer of the earth. where people are unhappy, and consequently interesting to a story-teller, he thinks he might get some information out of you.

Dick's comment alludes to two central strands in Victorian fiction, often intertwined and mutually supportive: the attempt to achieve a densely matted convincingness which ostensibly offers the reader an indubitable depiction of a believably 'real' world (its 'local colour' authentic), and a concern with the fate of individuals, their personal trajectories from unhappiness to happiness, or sometimes *vice-versa*. Both these facets of nineteenth-century fiction—which one might label, in shorthand, 'realism' and 'romance'—are criticised more explicitly elsewhere in the text. When Walter, in Chapter 24, has an unhappy story to tell he eschews any convincing density of detail, any nuanced elaboration, offering us only the bones, the basic shape of the tale: 'I will make it short enough, though I dare say it might be spun out into a long one, as used to be done with such subjects in the old novels'—and Morris's own compression of a whole historical novel, on 'how the change came', into a mere thirty pages (Chapters 17 and 18) perhaps exemplifies the same impatience with 'the long novel', a concern for the clearly intelligible structure of events rather than the vivid picturing and complex patterning of incidents.[6] Old Hammond's answer to Clara in Chapter 16 is even more directly sceptical of the 'realist' programme:

> It is true that in the nineteenth century, when there was so little art and so much talk about it, there was a theory that art and imaginative literature ought to deal with contemporary life; but they never did so; for, if there

[6] This is not to deny that this sketch of the process of the socialist revolution in England is, in some of its political and strategic details, remarkably specific, but a full analysis is impossible here.

> was any pretence of it, the author always took care . . to disguise, or exaggerate, or idealise, and in some way or other make it strange; so that, for all the verisimilitude there was, he might just as well have dealt with the times of the Pharaohs.

In Chapter 22 Ellen is complementarily contemptuous of novelists who selectively focus on the fate of privileged people:

> I say flatly that in spite of all their cleverness and vigour, and capacity for story-telling, there is something loathsome about them. Some of them. indeed, do here and there show some feeling for those whom the history-books call 'poor', and of the misery of whose lives we have some inkling; but presently they give it up, and towards the end of the story we must be contented to see the hero and heroine living happily in an island of bliss on other people's troubles; and that after a long series of sham troubles (or mostly sham) of their own making, illustrated by dreary intro-spective nonsense about their feelings and aspirations, and all the rest of it; while the world must even then have gone on its way, and dug and sewed and baked and built and carpentered round about these useless-animals.

Ellen's outburst is a response to her grandfather's admiration for nineteenth-century fiction; ironically, Morris so formulates this conservative defence of Victorian art as to make it suggest a quasi-'marxist'emphasis on the connection between the economic structure of a society and its fiction and also hint at a possible ideological distortion of the past when viewed through literary spectacles:

> I have read not a few books of the past days, and certainly they are much more alive than those which are written now; and good sound unlimited competition was the condition under which they were written—if we didn't know that from the record of history, we should know it from the books themselves. There is a spirit of

adventure in them, and signs of a capacity to extract good from evil which our literature quite lacks now; and I cannot help thinking that our moralists and historians exaggerate hugely the unhappiness of the past days, in which such splendid works of imagination and intellect were produced.

The case against nineteenth-century fiction suggested in these comments would, obviously, have to be argued further; the implication that realist romance is 'reactionary' is not elaborated, but at least Morris indicates that his hostile stance is not merely a temperamental response—though it is well known that he was personally blind to the great achievements of European realism and much preferred the saga and epics of older civilisations.[7]

Given these comments and this attitude to 'realism', it is clear that Morris, in writing *News*, is not setting out to rival the great realists in their own terms. It is also unlikely, I presume, that anyone would attempt to read, let alone judge, *News* according to the canons of 'realism'. It is perhaps worth elaborating a point made earlier: a critic who attempted to treat the 'characters' in *News* along lines similar to, for example, the way Stuart Hutchinson discusses the characters in James's *The Portrait of a Lady*—in terms of their motivations and decisions, their genuine comparability to the complexity of people we might know outside of fiction—would be deeply and obviously mistaken.[8]

Equally, another aspect of the kind of critical analysis which has derived from James's own practice, as novelist and critic, would seem curiously inapposite in a discussion of *News*. What I have in mind is that kind of criticism which regards the literary work as to be discussed primarily in terms of its formal qualities, so that an article on *The Portrait*

---

[7] On Morris as a literary critic, cf. Paul Thompson, ch. 8; for Morris's list of his 'Best Books'—and his dismissive comments on James—cf. E. P. Thompson, 1977 edition, pp. 659-60

[8] Cf Stuart Hutchinson, 'Beyond the Victorians: *The Portrait of a Lady*,' in *Reading the Victorian Novel: Detail into Form*, ed. Ian Gregor, ch 14, the essay which immediately preceded this contribution on Morris in the same volume.

almost inevitably subordinates any consideration of the moral dilemmas explored in that novel to a commentary on James's 'handling' of those dilemmas. The fine line which divides these two emphases may even be the subject of *Portrait* itself (the relation between James's use of 'portrait' and Wells's half-accurate accusation that 'life isn't a studio' would be relevant here—though Wells fails to register that it is surely James's characters who sometimes see life as a studio), but it is a fine line which haunts any critic influenced by James or by Leavis.

The obverse side of this point is that perhaps any novelist who strives for the kind of complex and nuanced unity inculcated by James will be drawn towards the microcosmic (the terrain of individuals, of moral subtleties, of personal and close relations), but be less able to deal with. to encompass adequately, the different complexities—and simplicities—of social and political movements. The absence of convincingly political novels within the English great tradition is germane here (one immediately thinks of the limitations of *Daniel Deronda*). Insofar as *News from Nowhere* both attempts to provoke discussion, inescapably, about its political content and tries to cope with the whole social and political domain, it was almost bound to be found wanting by Jamesian critical standards, and, conversely, to find Jamesian novelistic practice inadequate or inappropriate to its purpose.

Yet at the same time *News* doesn't offer itself as simply a socialist tract, a reverse variation on the purely didactic 'cautionary tale' so beloved of Victorian propagandists against the tastes, habits and aspirations of the 'lower classes'. It offers itself as a story, as fiction, and as the work of an artist, a craftsman with words who was, within a few years, to be seriously suggested as the successor to Tennyson as Poet Laureate. Clearly, *News* has to be classed more with the flood of tract publications than with *Daniel Deronda* or *Portrait*, yet its peculiar mingling of didactic intent with a kind of one-dimensional but vivid imagining might remind us rather of the conventions of cartoon-art or perhaps even of the strategies of satire.

If we were to regard *News* as, in a way, the 'obverse' of a satire, as depicting the 'norm' which would operate covertly or implicitly in a political satire, the relation of the text to both the details of the Victorian society it distances itself from, and to the principles which structure any capitalist society—competitiveness, antagonism, private profit-seeking, exchange-value, rather than collaboration, mutual help, communal benefit, use-value—might be somewhat clearer. Its own relation as a literary text to the local devices and general principles of 'realist' fiction might even be discussed along analogous lines.

However, rather than seek to 'categorise' *News* it seems more fruitful to take the hint offered not only by the content of the comments on nineteenth-century fiction quoted earlier but also by the very fact of their being included within the text itself, and to explore the effect of that inclusion on our awareness that there do indeed seem to be elements of both 'realism' and 'romance' in *News* itself. A way of putting the point would be that our awareness of some of the 'formal' aspects of *News* may even be part of its political "content'. One effect of these comments is to enforce some critical reflection on the reader's part about the text he or she is actually reading and its relation to a perhaps more familiar fare in fiction; the reader, faced with these comments, is necessarily reminded that *News from Nowhere* is also a fiction, yet insofar as it dissociates itself from the fiction of its own period it appears to demand to be read in a different kind of way.[9] It is this prompted doubleness of response that invites analysis, and it is convenient to focus on two aspects: the formal function of detail and the process of reading.

*

[9] Other instances of the text being aware of its own fictiveness include the Laurence Sterne-like Chapter 13, 'Concerning Politics'. Even the title, in the pages of *Commonweal*, would indicate a certain playfulness.

The opening chapter is an intriguing instance of how the reader's response can be made peculiarly ambivalent by the details offered. The first words of the text, 'Up at the League, says a friend', begin a pattern of oscillations in the rest of the chapter, with variations on the phrase 'says a friend' intrusively and, it might seem, awkwardly repeated. As we read we treat this "friend' as a transparent device, collapsing the "friend', the 'he' about whom the friend speaks, and the authorial voice itself into one, and that one is clearly to be taken as William Morris himself. That multiple identification is almost, but not quite, admitted at the close of the chapter:

> Our friend says that from that sleep he awoke once more, and afterwards went through such surprising adventures that he thinks that they should be told to our comrades and indeed the public in general and therefore proposes to tell them now. But, says he, I think it would be better if I told them in the first person, as if it were myself who had gone through them; which, indeed, will be the easier and more natural to me, since I understand the feelings and desires of the comrade of whom I am telling better than any one else in the world does.

The effect is curious: we almost over-react to the obviousness of the device, the grammar of shifting pronouns almost tempts us into so eluding their refusal of first-person attribution that we end up almost believing that when the 'I' does finally speak in its own voice that 'I' is telling a reluctant truth rather than organising a fiction; yet at the same time the very clumsiness of the authorial prevarications reminds us emphatically that this is indeed fiction despite the circumstantial and autobiographical authenticity of what we are told: the League, the debates, the tube-train, the station five miles walk from the house on the Thames, the new suspension bridge (built by Bazalgette in 1887), all have a real and documentable existence in the London of 1890. This opening chapter already establishes a fluctuating relation between the text and the 'real' which is to permeate the whole work.

Some other moments of definite reference to the extra-textual 'real' can be simply listed: the location of the guest-house on the site of Morris's own Hammersmith home, the mention of the Hammersmith Socialists in Chapter 3, the memories of actual childhood in Epping Forest included in the same chapter, the final detailed description of Kelmscott Manor (Morris's Oxfordshire home) in the last chapters, including comments on his own work ('still hung with old tapestries, originally of no artistic value'). Such moments are obviously aspects of the general device of superimposing the imagined future directly onto a present topography intimately known, and this is, of course, a variation on familiar realist techniques (Hardy's Wessex and Dickens's London map easily but not exactly onto their respective actual terrains), though the geographical details act in this text as a constant reminder of the very fictiveness of the work: it is the disparity as much as the identity, the departure from reality as well as the accurate observation, that we are constantly invited to recognise.

Such a strategy of juxtaposition, of direct contrast between the actual now and the imagined possibility, is basic to any Utopian fiction, but Morris's text brings the two worlds 'physically' much closer together than any previous Utopia. Almost all Utopian societies before Bellamy's *Looking Backward* had been located in a geographical elsewhere,[10] and even Bellamy's Boston is utterly unrecognisable, whereas Morris's future England occupies exactly the same geographical terrain as the England of 1890. Guest's route from 26 Upper Mall, Hammersmith, to Bedford Square and the British Museum (ch. 4 to ch. 8) can easily be traced in detail in a *London A-Z*—and the exercise is revealing: names like Primrose Hill and Kensington Gardens sound new notes.[11] The closeness of the physical identification between the now and the then serves to make

10 Cf. Meier, vol. I, Part Two for a survey of previous Utopian works.

11 It is perhaps also worth noting that the river-trip in *News* traverses much the same well-known territory as that in the widely-popular *Three Men in a Boat*, published in 1889

more possible, more tantalisingly near, more credible, this transformed world and yet simultaneously reminds us poignantly of its remoteness, its fictional status. The recognition that the 'large open space, sloping somewhat toward the south, the sunny site of which had been taken advantage of for planting an orchard' (in Chapter 7) is actually Trafalgar Square, with all its associations of 13 November 1887 ('Bloody Sunday', also echoed in ch. 17), is one sharp instance of this doubleness of vision.

In this use of geographical detail Morris is clearly very close to certain tactics of realism yet we are being prompted to read such details in a directly political way, to be alert to their political implications. At times we are reminded that some elements of this future, gracious society are already present, albeit distorted or hidden, in the old 'now': the description of the beautiful country-side of the upper Thames, which remains beautiful across the centuries, juxtaposed with comments on the nineteenth-century country-houses as having been 'mere blots on the face of the land' (ch. 29), is one instance of this effect on a large scale, while the Pevsner-like mention of the *Fleur-de-lis* on the village guest-house (ch. 27) is a miniature example of the revealing and mellowing change that time itself can bring to something the beauty of which is now obscured to us.

At other times a descriptive detail can pull us up sharply, as we register the historical and political distance that has been travelled. Guest's own reaction to the bridge in Chapter 2 is the paradigm of this, but a single adjective can have the same effect: that the garden in front of the Thames-side houses is 'continuous' (ch. 2) indicates a very radical shift in property-values. The significance of such 'local' details is self-consciously underlined for us in the explanation, in Chapter 25, as to why there are numerous birds of prey in the air (no more gamekeepers, no more game-laws, no more landed gentry . . .); Guest's working this out for himself ('did not even have to ask Dick') is obviously a nudge to the reader to think about the implications of similar 'realistic' details.

As we read *News* we do indeed find ourselves noting apparently realistic touches with an awareness of the questions and problems they raise, their presence registered not so much as 'convincing' (or otherwise) but as indicating the carefulness (or otherwise) of the author's political imagination, the precision of his political thinking. A list of various kinds of bread can prompt us to ponder on the overseas links and foreign trade of this society ('the thin pipe-stems of wheaten crust, such as I have eaten in Turin', ch. 3). A comment that the road-menders' clothes, gleaming with "gold and silk embroidery', are 'under the guardianship of a six-year-old boy, who had his arm thrown over the neck of a big mastiff' (ch. 7) can set the mind racing back and forth on the problem of personal possessions and casual theft. That the road-menders have a 'fore-man' raises the old queries of the Anarchist. That Dick, talking about children's education in Chapter 5, rather casually plays down 'book-learning' helps us to note the detail in Chapter 6 that both the shop-children are reading books—and that Dick himself in Chapter 8 knows Shakespeare well enough to recall the Bishop of Ely's house in *Richard II*. Morris is at times explicit about *not* offering a solution to a problem raised by a detail: a minor instance is the good Rhine wine in Chapter 6 ('I made a mental note to ask Dick how they managed to make fine wine . . '); a more substantial one is the absence of any explanation of the form of fuel or power for the 'orce-vehicles' (ch. 24).

Our sense that we have to read with an eye open to the underlying political ramifications of such details is itself part of a wider awareness of the artificial nature of the text, our sense of the presence of Morris prompting us rather than trying to 'convince' us—and at times that prompting becomes a kind of playing with us: we find ourselves watching with amusement as Morris quite blatantly works into the text various side-hits at his own pet aversions.[12] For example, the coins with which Guest tries to pay Dick are

[12] In his review of Bellamy's *Looking Backward*, which provided the immediate stimulus for writing *News*, Morris remarked that 'the only safe way of reading a Utopia is to consider it as the expression of the temperament of its author'; cf. May Morris, *William Morris: Artist, Writer, Socialist* (Oxford, 1936), vol. II, p. 502.

there not only as signs of the time-shift (oxidised) or of the abolition of the cash-nexus but also, mischievously, to provoke Dick's rather gratuitously insulting remarks on their ugliness compared to those of Edward III's reign (ch. 2). When we are given a glimpse of the Houses of Parliament (in 1890 the largest new building in England since the Reformation) they have, predictably, been turned into 'a storage place for manure'—Morris in 1888 had fought a long struggle against the League's Parliamentarians, and he had Dickens's backing for the imagery of 'manure'; but the preservation of the building itself is owing to 'a queer antiquarian society which had done some service in past times', and we realise that Morris's own Anti-Scrape activities have borne ironic fruit. Such moments link us back to those opening realistic details about Morris's own life and remind us of the connections between this future society and his present political activities ('Up at the League . .'), which include, of course, the writing of this very fiction we are reading.

None of these various uses of detail could be exactly paralleled within the confines of a text modelled according to a realist aesthetic, even though many of them at first glance offer themselves as authenticating the 'reality' of the world presented. It is clear that to attempt to read *News* as trying to build up a convincing picture or realistic representation of a future society would be to mistake the significance of such details: they lead outwards from the text towards an idea of, and arguments about, such a society, rather than inwards to a depth or density of close-meshed fictional coherence which then offers itself as a 'real' depiction of a 'real' world. Obviously, then, faced with the absence of, say, any sustained account of the processes of heavy industry (a preoccupation of some marxist futurologists), we need not regard this as a gaping and disabling hole in the Utopian picture; we simply recognise that the text is not concerned to present a seamlessly complete 'world' but rather to indicate the essential elements of an adequately human society. What those essential elements are, for Morris, is best approached obliquely by a consideration of another facet of the text: the interplay between romance elements and the process of reading.

The defining characteristics of the new society are sketched in very early in the text. As Guest approaches the waterman, in Chapter 2, 'he nodded to me, and bade me good morning as if he expected me'; as Guest gets back into the boat after his over-brief swim, the waterman 'held out his hand to help me'; once Guest looks closely at the waterman he notices that he had 'a peculiarly pleasant and friendly look about his eyes.' Such details could, of course, occur in a description of a real event or pass without comment in a realist novel, as minor contributions to characterisation. Here they carry a different weight, as indicating the habits and norms of the new society: it is in the attitudes, tones, expressions, of people that the basic beauty of this future life is to be found. George Orwell begins his account of Republican Spain, in *Homage to Catalonia*, with a glimpse of that possible life in a casual encounter:

> As we went out he stepped across the room and gripped my hand very hard. Queer, the affection you can feel for a stranger! It was as though his spirit and mine had momentarily succeeded in bridging the gulf of language and tradition and meeting in utter intimacy. I hoped he liked me as well as I liked him. But I also knew that to retain my first impression of him I must not see him again; and needless to say I never did see him again. One was always making contacts of that kind in Spain.

In the communist England of the twenty-second century the quality of such contacts—'the affection you can feel for a stranger'— defines the habitual and basic relations between everyone.

The point should be obvious, but it also opens up onto the overall structure of the work: not only is such 'affection' part of the world suggested to us, it also provides the principle by which our relation as readers to the text is organised and controlled, and so too, in an interesting way, does the notion of never seeing the 'stranger' again. It is clear from the third chapter that the women Guest encounters fascinate him: of the three women in the guest-house 'one of them (was) very handsome' and this "handsome one', Annie, later 'stood behind me with her hand on my shoulder'—a gesture that would clearly break the codes of high Victorian propriety governing meetings between strangers of the opposite sex! As the exchange about Guest's age proceeds, we can feel his interest in this 'pretty girl', and we recognise the undertones of desire when he comments 'She blushed a little under my gaze, though it was clear that she had taken me for a man of eighty"—that inconsequential 'though' speaks loudly of silent wishes on Guest's part. When she leaves the room she takes "at least part of the sun' with her. Annie's appearance and her—for Guest—too premature disappearance, suggests the pattern which is to follow.

In Chapter 4, on the way to Bloomsbury, Guest notices 'a beautiful woman, tall, dark-haired, and white-skinned . . who smiled kindly on me and more kindly still, I thought, on Dick'—that touch of male envy is to be picked up later. Her passing presence distracts him till she disappears from view—'and I felt that disappointed kind of feeling which overtakes one when one has seen an interesting or lovely face in the streets which one is never likely to see again. ' In Chapter 6 'the pretty Annie' is briefly remembered, then Guest is quickly attracted by yet another 'very handsome woman', who agrees to look after the horse while Dick and Guest shop. Guest's admiration this time is more explicit and prompts the comment from Dick: "'Tis a good job there are so many of them that every Jack may have his Jill." But when they come out of the shop, 'to my disappointment, like a change in a dream, a tall old man was holding our horse instead of the beautiful woman'. As the journey continues, Guest takes note of more 'young girls' and women, and we are also made aware that Dick is hoping to meet someone 'whom I particularly want to see', his blush indicating whom: Clara, who appears in Chapter 9. This, the first chapter given over to Old Hammond's long exposition of the new society and its history, is titled 'Concerning Love', and Guest's first question when Hammond offers to answer 'questions about anything' is not concerned with economics or politics but simply: "That beautiful girl, is he (Dick) going to be married to her?" That Guest has his priorities right becomes increasingly clear as the work proceeds.

We can return, briefly, to Old Hammond, later, but it is the emergence of Guest's interest in the women of the new society, as a major strand in the construction of the text, that I want to pursue. That interest remains focussed on Clara during the meal in Chapter 16 ('I thought it bad manners to stare at Clara all the time, though she was quite worth it'), but on the return to Hammersmith it is Annie who again attracts him: 'Annie shook hands with me, and hoped I had had a pleasant day—so kindly that I felt a slight pang as our hands parted; for to say the truth I liked her better than Clara' (ch. 20). He falls asleep that night with a 'vague fear'—but awakes still in the future, and Annie is the first person he meets; she 'gave me a kiss, quite meaningless I fear except as betokening friendship' (ch. 21); but Annie soon disappears again, left behind as the journey up-river begins, though her parting kiss 'almost took away from me my desire for that expedition.'

The immediately following chapter provides him with a new focus of attraction, in Ellen (echoes of course of Helen), and the terms of admiration are even stronger: 'her strange and almost wild beauty. ' Chapter 23 suggests hovering complications between Dick and Clara and Ellen, and Guest's male envy and sense of being *de trop* are heavily marked ('I hope you see that you have left me out of the tale'), but Chapter 24 returns to the pattern: Ellen is left behind—and 'quite a keen pang smote me as I thought how I should never see the beautiful girl again.' Ellen does however reappear, in Chapter 27 (the delay being filled with Walter Allen's tale of jealousy), and she thereby seems to be breaking the pattern—though initially Guest fears that her arrival is prompted by affection for Dick.

Guest's subsequent relation with Ellen need not be traced in detail; the growth of his love for her is clear, as is his fear of losing her. And in the end, of course, in returning to the nineteenth century, he does indeed lose her: Ellen's is the last face he sees from the future before ('like a change in a dream') he encounters, shocked, the apparently old labourer. That final loss of Ellen is, as we have seen, the last, and worst, of a series of disappointments related to women, but whereas the earlier brief encounters and the suddenly curtailed relation with Annie are held within a frame of promise, of possible re-encounter or resumed relation, or at least another 'Jill', the separation from Ellen is sharp and final. It is a curious ending by certain standards—precisely those standards of 'happy ending' criticised by Ellen herself. Few novels which rest so much on a gradually developing love-interest would conclude on such an arbitrary separation—even Utopian fictions tend to ensure that the explorer of Utopia finally marries the inevitable heroine (Bellamy's Julian West, Butler's narrator).

Yet Morris's ending is not a simply arbitrary one, nor is it absolutely dictated by the notion of time-travel: Bellamy had found a technical solution to those problems and his devices might have been improved upon— Wells's *The Time Machine* was to be written in 1894. The constant teasing or tantalising of the reader by the pattern of aroused but frustrated attraction and involvement, of which the loss of Ellen is the culmination, is crucial to the political impact of the book. in at least two aspects. The reader, insofar as he or she has 'identified with' the love-relation between Guest and Ellen and has willed its consummation (in accordance with the familiar expectations of popular and naive 'romance'), is left by the ending with a final feeling of frustration.

That frustration thereby serves to provoke a desire that, *nevertheless*, that relationship might be achieved—but that doesn't mean only, in Brecht's ambiguous phrase, 'rewriting the ending'.[13] It means endeavouring, outside the anti-climax of the tale, to achieve the kind of society where such a relationship might be possible, it means re-establishing that future. In a curious but definite way, the desire of the lover (and by transference the desire of the reader) is coupled with, brought into the service of, the political desire that the text seeks to provoke—and the text itself makes precisely

[13] Bertolt Brecht, *The Good Woman of Setsuan*, Epilogue.

that connection explicit: 'Looking back now, we can see that the great motive-power of the change was a longing for freedom and equality, akin if you please to the unreasonable passion of the lover' (ch. 17).

By this abrupt and *un*-satisfying ending, we are left by the novel in a state akin to that of the narrator in the first chapter: 'I understood the feelings and desires of the comrade of whom' I have been reading. I, too, if I am a reader attuned to the patterns of 'popular romance' fiction, have been drawn, perhaps reluctantly, like the opening narrator, into the text and my expulsion from it leaves an unfulfilled desire, a lost object I seek to re-discover in the non-fictional world that remains when the text has closed in upon itself.

Secondly, and closely linked to this effect, is a more dispersed desire played upon by the text, a desire for the *kind* of (love-)relationships that seem possible in the future world—for it is a change in human relations rather than in forces of production (though the former is clearly not possible without the latter, as Old Hammond's account makes explicit) that characterises the new society as communist. Those relations are seen in the guest-house, in the shop and street, in every working activity, they are palpable in the touch of hands and the expressions on faces, and what is at the core of those relations is the promise of a gift: the society of *News from Nowhere* is a. gift-society in the fullest sense[14] —and the most basic and 'Utopian' gift-relationship is precisely that of love.

In making of his text a kind of finally with-held gift of satisfaction Morris is utilising a device familiar to psychoanalysis—this text, too, is a game of *Fort/Da* [15]—and in putting sexual relations at the heart of his Utopian fiction Morris is discovering for himself an insight into

---

[14] Cf. the development of Marcel Mauss's notion of 'the gift' in Richard M. Titmuss, *The Gift Relationship* (London, 1970)

[15] Cf. S. Freud, *Beyond the Pleasure Principle* (1920), *Standard Edition*, vol. XVIII, p. 14f.

‘communism’ which—appropriately—the young Marx had had:[16]

> The immediate, natural, necessary relation of human being to human being is the relationship of man to woman. In this natural species-relationship the relation of man to nature is immediately his relation to man. Just as his relation to man is immediately his relation to nature, his own natural condition. Therefore this relationship reveals in a sensuous form, reduced to an observable fact, the extent to which the human essence has become nature for man or nature has become the human essence for man. It is possible to judge from this relationship the entire level of development of mankind. . . This relationship also demonstrates the extent to which man's needs have become human needs, hence the extent to which the other, as a human being, has become a need for him, the extent to which in his most individual existence he is at the same time a communal being.

We can now draw some strands together and, very briefly, suggest a wider argument. It is clear that the device of enticing, or teasing, the reader into a frustrated desire which might provoke political displace-ment of that desire rests not only on certain romance conventions but also on the overt fictiveness of the text itself. The appropriate reaction is effected because we know that the work is *not* offered to us as a ‘real’ account, in which the ending lies outside our control and—by a deep convention of realism—apparently outside that of the author too (the ‘inevitability’ effect), but rather as a deliberate and challenging demand upon us, a demand we can ignore only if we treat the text as

---

[16] K. Marx. 'Economic and Philosophical Manuscripts' (1844), in *Early Writings* (Pelican Marx Library, 1975), p. 347. The obvious problem of the retention of male dominance in *News from Nowhere*—or Marx's use of the term ‘man’ for humanity—can be debated some other time.

a different and more familiar kind of fiction, as indeed 'pure fiction'. Yet at the same time, in playing variations on the realist use of detail and in utilising, in its own structure of expectations, one of the primary components of the pleasure of reading romance fiction, *News from Nowhere* is clearly, in these aspects, at least a second-cousin to the tradition from which it dissociates itself.

In other aspects, of course, *News from Nowhere* makes a much sharper break with the conventions of nineteenth-century fiction: the expository chapters given over to Old Hammond loom large in our reading experience (and in familiar objections to the work). There is, as one could show, a certain element of teasing here too—in the arrangement of this long discourse and in the fact of it being there at all. But the essential point to make is that once 'organicist' or 'Jamesian' criteria of fiction are left aside and we read rather with an awareness of fictiveness, of the conventions of fiction—some older than the nineteenth century (the long discourses in Homer, the sagas, the Old Testament), some established in twentieth-century fiction (the long argumentative conversations in *Magic Mountain* or *The Glass Bead Game*)—the eighty or so pages devoted to Old Hammond need cause no more of a formal problem than catechetical exposition does in Plato.[17] The specific content of these chapters may well arouse different degrees of interest in different readers, but in 1890 (after Bellamy's success) and in the pages of *Commonweal*, Morris could presume a high level of prior interest.

But, of course, the critical objection is often to the 'awkward' inclusion of these chapters in an otherwise mainly, if thinly and unsuccessfully, 'realist' work—by which is meant the latter half of the tale. Yet, as I have tried to suggest, both the realist and the romance elements in *News* are so handled that the overt fictiveness of the text modifies our response to them in a self-reflexive way; we are made aware of them as conventions of fiction which are being

---

[17] Morris's tactic is worth comparing with Mallock's in his *The New Republic*—which also, it seems, influenced Wells's *Boon*, the immediate occasion for the break with James.

manipulated by the author for purposes which stand askew to the familiar effects of fiction. The Old Hammond chapters can then be seen as another instance of this acknowledgement of the limits, and the undermining of the conventions of, 'Victorian fiction': we are being invited to recognise that since so much of fiction is implicitly didactic, we might as well settle back and read some explicitly didactic exposition. These chapters, one might say, bring together Morris's equivalent of all those quasi-authorial comments on morals, the organisation of society and common sense wisdom which operate as the voice of truth in the hierarchy of voices that constitutes the realist mode.[18]

In certain respects, then, we can see that *News from Nowhere* comes close to some of the preoccupations of 'modernist' fiction: there is the same sense of the artefact declaring itself as made, constructed, self-conscious of its own devices; there is an element of using the conventions of fiction as part of its own material; there is a playing upon the relation of the reader to the text as a text rather than as a depiction of a world.[19] Clearly, *News* is not a modernist masterpiece before its time, but we can now read it with a certain hind-sight and recognise in its mingling of conventions and its self-awareness, its deliberate breaking of certain expectations, its cavalier attitude to the pre-occupations of other nineteenth-century novelists, a serious response to the dominant tradition of fiction in its own day.

We should also, obviously, recall the more basic point about *News*, that Morris was content to bracket it with his historical handbook for militants, *Socialism: its growth and outcome*, as a 'more or less propagandist' work.[20] The fact that

---

[18] For a sketch of the analysis of ''realism' implied here cf. Colin MacCabe, 'Realism and the Cinema: Notes on some Brechtian theses', *Screen*, vol. 15, no. 2 (Summer 1974), pp. 7-10.

[19] A certain congruence between Morris's preference for pre-Renaissance literature and elements of 'modernism' in his own fiction is perhaps not surprising, in view of the general argument advanced in Gabriel Josipovici's *The World and the Book* (London, 1971).

[20] Meier, vol. I, p. 268. citing a letter from Morris to Hyndman, (22 Dec) 1890.

a work of fiction intended primarily as a contribution to militant socialist propaganda should have challenged and tried to both undermine and modify some of the conventions of fiction need not surprise us if we remember that in all of Morris's many activities —his work in textiles, tapestry, embroidery, wall-papers, furniture, stained-glass, printing, architecture—he was constantly aware of the relation between the formal qualities of a work of art and its social, and finally political, use.

It was from Ruskin that Morris. in his early Pre-Rapahelite Brotherhood days, first learned that the relation between detail and form is always politically significant. Two years after writing *News* he reprinted on the Kelmscott Press that crucial chapter of *Stones of Venice*, 'The Nature of Gothic'. And forty years after Morris, Brecht too was to recognise that a political challenge necessarily involves an aesthetic challenge, and he too set out—more explicitly, more coherently, and more successfully—to create a political propagandist art which was aware of its own devices, its own artificiality, and which took as its material not only the political dilemmas of its day but also the popular and dominant forms of art, precisely in order to undermine them.

A brief essay can only sketch a case, but—to use again Morris's own words in his review of Bellamy[21]—though it may still be true that 'to anyone not deeply interested in the social question it could not be at all an attractive book', it may also be possible for a critic to find interesting both the 'serious essay' and the 'slight envelope of romance' in *News from Nowhere*, since in important aspects of the text—and not least the deliberate slightness of the envelope— the two cannot finally be separated.

*

---

21 My opening quotation is taken from that review, cf. May Morris, vol. II, pp. 501-2. Considering Morris's own concern with the criteria of 'care and art' in literature, it would indeed be surprising if he had merely lapsed into the same faults he had criticised in Bellamy.

TRESSELL AND THE TRUTHS OF FICTION[1]

Let me begin with what may appear to be a detour. My subject is 'Tressell and the truths of fiction' — but for me that title has a silent question-mark at the end of it, a note of query about the very idea of fiction having or offering 'truths'. My initial detour will attempt to explain why.

In his own Tressell Memorial Lecture, in 1982, Raymond Williams, explaining his preferred title of the book as *The Ragged-Arsed Philanthropists*, said this:

> I have a sore point about the title because I was prevented, for many years, from reading this extraordinary book in its then reduced edition, because I took it, from knowledge of its title alone, to be one of those maudlin Victorian tracts which showed that it didn't matter how poor you were, you could always help others, and I'd assumed—I suppose I shouldn't have—that it would be a sentimental tale of people down on their luck who were helping others . . .

I begin with Williams' admission about how long it took him to get over that title and actually read the book partly because my own talk is meant to be a kind of memorial for Raymond Williams as well as for Tressell; much of what I want to say will be in various ways indebted to Williams. And partly because I have an even more damaging admission to make: that I was put off for a very long time from reading *The Ragged Trousered Philanthropists* not just because of its title but simply because it was a novel. It wasn't in fact until after I'd seen a dramatic adaptation of the novel, by the Joint Stock Theatre Company in 1978, that I finally opened the book, though I'd bought a copy several years before. Since I assume that most of you will probably have read and re-read this novel that we are here to celebrate, you may well feel that my long reluctance to read it at all makes me an inappropriate memorialist.

[1] The Robert Tressell Memorial Lecture, Queen's Hotel, Hastings, 1988.

But my reluctance wasn't, as I say, due to any specific prejudice against Tressell, but to a general prejudice against the very form of the novel—an odd prejudice for somebody who, after all, teaches English—but one not untypical of my 'generation'. My detour is to attempt to explain that prejudice by offering a brief contrast between Raymond Williams's generation and my own.

Williams was born in 1921 and his formative political moments were, arguably, the 1926 General Strike (in retrospect, that is—he was only five at the time!), the years of the Depression, of Spain and the anti-Fascist struggle, of the Communist Party in the late 1930s, the War, and, crucially, the post-war Labour Government. Throughout those various moments, there was a strong, even overwhelming sense that the obvious and only place for a British socialist (in his case a Welsh socialist) was in the labour movement. Not necessarily, of course, in the Labour Party, but in some direct association and involvement with the organised working-class of this country. It was then an obvious route for him, on leaving Cambridge in 1946 or so, to take a job with the Oxford Delegacy, teaching in what was essentially a Workers' Educational Association context, based here in Hastings. Some of you, I hope, will remember him from those days. In 1961 he was transplanted back to Cambridge, with several books already written of what was to become the most impressive and wide-ranging body of socialist writing produced by any individual in this country since, arguably, William Morris. And throughout those years, and later, Williams was not only teaching and writing about novels but actually writing novels.

My own formation, twenty years later, was different. I was born in 1944, simultaneously with the Education Act which eventually enabled me—as a Liverpool working-class kid—to end up in Cambridge in the 1960s, where I first met Raymond Williams. I graduated in 1968, that turbulent year of the Paris 'Events' that is itself being so generally memorialised at present. On 1st May 1968, twenty years ago tomorrow, I was not, however, in Paris but at a launch meeting for the *May Day Manifesto*, edited by Williams. It was, nevertheless, that complex of events labelled "May '68" which was my decisive political formation and which indirectly—to come back to where we started—made me almost indifferent, for quite some time, to the reading of novels, including *The Ragged Trousered Philanthropists*. Yet I was, as a student, officially 'reading English'. Why the indifference? And what possible connection was there?

It's worth, I think, taking you on this brief detour through my life, because there's a large political and cultural issue lurking, to do with some still-active discontinuities between a kind of politics that in important respects could link Tressell and Williams and the political perspectives of that 1968 generation.

Let me put it this way. I did some research, on working-class autobiographies in the nineteenth century, but when I finally left Cambridge in 1971 I had three possible jobs or futures to choose between. One was a WEA job, in the Colne Valley or perhaps in Liverpool. I had put in for both posts and maybe would have had a chance of getting one. Second was an invitation to join a team in Central America, based in Guatemala, working with peasant organisations and, eventually, with various liberation struggles, including the Sandinistas in Nicaragua. Third was a possible job teaching English at the then fairly new University of Kent.

For me, the real choice was between the second and third options. The first—the WEA job in a traditional working-class territory, in close association, probably, with a local labour movement and Labour Party organisation—seemed, at the time, a kind of anachronism, no longer where a socialist politics was to be located. That wasn't just, I think, the arrogance of youth nor simply the anger at what, under Harold Wilson, the 'labour movement' had seemed to accept and even endorse: the acquiescence in American aggression in Vietnam, the failure to support African struggles against Smith and South Africa, the acceptance of an IMF view of the world, etc. The question could be put in this form: what, any longer, did the world of *The Ragged Trousered Philanthropists* have to say to me, a student socialist of '68, and why was I so unconcerned even to find out if it might have something to say? Part of the answer lies in the notion of the 'truths' of fiction.

In May 1968 there appeared an essay which was to be very influential upon people of my formation and situation. It was an immensely ambitious essay, entitled 'Components of the National Culture', written by Perry Anderson, then editor of *New Left Review*. [2] It tried to survey the whole range of British intellectual culture and to see why it operated as a block, as a stifling constraint upon the possibility of socialism in this country. It's a difficult essay to quote briefly from so I'll try and paraphrase parts of its argument.

In looking across the entire range of academic disciplines—history, philosophy, political studies, economics, anthropology, etc.—Anderson asked what characterised them, taken together, as the British intellectual culture. What he deliberately left out of his survey was any treatment of, on the one hand, literature, fiction, novels, and on the other the natural sciences. The grounds for this omission were that it was the area in-between, the disciplines of the social sciences, which gave us the very concepts by which we can think adequately about the world we live in. What fiction gave was not concepts at all, and what the natural sciences dealt with was not the human world we construct and live in but the world of physics, of nature.

If we look at those disciplines which should give us the means to understand that human world, what we find in England is a systematic refusal to think about the *whole* society. Each of those disciplines, those intellectual inquiries, took one fragment and deliberately refused to explore the connections with the other fragments: history had little to do with philosophy, economics ignored political theory, aesthetics was blind to economics, etc. What we needed, argued the essay, was a 'totalising'theory, a theory of society which tried to take on board the totality of where we live, all its aspects together. What in other intellectual traditions—in France, Germany, Italy—had provided that totalising theory was either Marxism or classical sociology, and that is precisely what British culture at its formal intellectual level excluded.

---

[2] *New Left Review,* No. 50; reprinted in *Student Power,* edited by Alexander Cockburn and Robin Blackburn, Penguin Books, 1969.

Instead, a curious gap or distortion appeared in that cultural terrain. What was trying to take the place of Marxism or sociology, what was trying to offer a kind of centre, a point from which the whole might be seen, was— of all things— literary criticism: the study of literature, of fictions. Anderson ended by pointing out that it wasn't therefore merely accidental that the leading British socialist thinker of his generation, Raymond Williams, had himself developed out of literary criticism. If there was one place in the English cultural scene where some attempt to see the whole had actually taken place, it was literary criticism— though it shouldn't have been.

But why couldn't literature, the writing and reading of novels, provide the centre of the intellectual culture? After all, hadn't the great nineteenth-century novels sought, precisely, to embrace the whole society, to offer a ''total' account? What else is *Middlemarch*? But Anderson argued, against this, that after the emergence of Marxism and of Freudian psychoanalysis we now had radically new ways of understanding ourselves, but as yet those new and difficult ways of understanding had not become naturalised and familiar to us. Nobody in ordinary life actually talks in Marxist or Freudian terms; their crucial analytical terms remain technical vocabularies. Those concepts which are central to the revolutionising of the way in which the twentieth century understands economy, family, power, society, have not yet been assimilated into the way we ordinarily talk about men and women, work and home. But since the novel form rests upon and uses as its most basic material our ordinary language, until people begin to speak in conceptually adequate ways about their society, no adequate post-Marx, post-Freud novel can be written.

Now, compare that case about the novel with the first critical book on Robert Tressell, which was published the following year, 1969: *Robert Tressell and the Ragged Trousered Philanthropists* by Jack Mitchell (with a foreword by, of course, Raymond Williams!). At one point Mitchell is talking about the Chartists' attempts to write socialist novels in the nineteenth century. What went wrong with those attempts, he says, was that they started from 'ideas', and a novel which starts from ideas and then tries, as it were, to dress them up in some form of story, is going to fail as a novel. Where you have to start from, for Jack Mitchell, and what he partly admires Tressell for, is with an absorbing curiosity about the men and women involved in struggle. If the 'artistic framework' is invented simply to illustrate a message, an idea, a concept, the book will fail as a novel (p. 31). Mitchell also claims that when you are reading a good novel, including Tressell's book, you "cease to look upon what is happening as a story set in the past; [the reader] becomes involved in the action going on before his eyes as he would in something unfinished, something contemporary to him in his own life. ' (p. 67) And for Mitchell one of Tressell's merits is that his 'narrative prose is plain, sober, concrete—a 'clear glass, or rather lens, through which the reader views reality. ' (p. 64)

Each of these positions offered by Mitchell—the involvement in the story as real, the prose as a clear glass, fiction as being dependent not on ideas but on curiosity about people—I would have rejected at that time, for reasons which have political as well as literary or critical importance. Yet Mitchell's way of talking about novels does, in England, seem the 'obvious' way to think about 'reading a novel'. There is, in fact, a basic divergence here, not only between two moments or positions within the culture but also between two kinds of politics.

What followed from Anderson's analysis was the need for totalising concepts, for an overall theory which could build upon and bring together the innovating languages of Marx and Freud, as a basis for grasping, understanding, and thereby beginning to change, the whole of society. The basic political contrast here was, of course, with the deeply 'pragmatic' and 'commonsensical'approach of the leaders of the Labour Party and of most trades unions—in other words, a profound refusal to think about the *interrelations* between, say, wage demands and foreign policy, racism and exports, sexism and unemployment, media ownership and inflation, nuclear weapons and education. Each of these, in the perspective of conventional British politics, was only to be 'tackled' in terms of an essentially short-term and incremental approach, a matter of marginal reform, of single issue campaigns. The contrast with the total social change of the various Third World revolutions, or with the scope of the original Marxist project, or with the ambitious overall analysis of the *May Day Manifesto*, was clear. In the wake of Anderson's argument, and his editorial policy at *New Left Review*, therefore, a whole generation of British socialist intellectuals spent nearly a decade trying to arrive at (or simply import from Continental thinkers) such totalising concepts and theories. It was an extraordinary period, looking back, and it helped to confirm a fissure between two sides of what could have been one movement.

One of the ambitions of that period, among many of my contemporaries, was to arrive not only at a theory of the social totality but specifically at a *theory* of literature—a theory in which the 'commonsensical' attitude to literature was itself seen as something to be guarded against, as a dangerous fiction, and in which Jack Mitchell's way of reading was seen as collusive with those dangers. What was needed, as with any other area of social practice, was to analyse, to dismantle, the literary text, not to believe in its reality: to understand a fiction as a construction of effects, not to respond to it as 'a gallery of memorable characters'.

Let me try to illustrate the argument of that perspective by analysing the text of *The Ragged Trousered Philanthropists* itself. First, Tressell's own Preface to the book. He very firmly makes Mitchell's kind of distinction:

> . . *The Philanthropists* is not a treatise or essay, but a novel. My main object was to write a readable story full of human interest and based upon the happenings of everyday life, the subject of Socialism being treated incidentally. This was the task I set myself. To what extent I have succeeded is for others to say; but whatever their verdict, the work possesses at least one merit—that of being true. I have invented nothing. There are no scenes or incidents in the story that I have

> not either witnessed myself or had conclusive evidence of.

For Tressell here it seems that the 'truth' of fiction lies in his not having invented anything—in other words in it not being fiction, made up, at all. Yet he wants to insist that it's a novel, a story, not an essay or a treatise. What this almost-contradictory claim invites, within the perspective of a theory of literature, is an analysis of how the effect of 'truth'might be created by a novel, by the writing in that novel operating not as a 'clear glass' but as a dense mesh of deliberate devices, each achieving a local but also cumulative *effect* of 'truth' and in so doing eliding that very distinction, and strain, between truth and invention.

If we now look at the first chapter of Tressell's novel we can see how he used some of the standard devices of novelists to give that effect of truth. Here's the first paragraph:

> The house was named "The Cave". It was a large old-fashioned three-storied building standing in about an acre of ground, and situated about a mile outside the town of Mugsborough. It stood back nearly two hundred yards from the main road and was reached by means of a by-road or lane, on each side of which was a hedge formed of hawthorn trees and blackberry bushes. This house had been unoccupied for many years and it was now being altered and renovated for its new owner by the firm of Rushton & Co. Builders and Decorators, [p. 13 / p. 15] [3]

A standard kind of opening. You describe something in exactly the way you would describe it if it were really in front of you. There is (almost) no trace here that this is fiction—and that is itself the deepest convention of the dominant

---

[3] I have mainly quoted from my own battered and abridged copy, published by The Richards Press in 1954, but for convenience I have given page references to the Lawrence & Wishart 1955 edition and then to the Grafton paperback edition.

form of the novel: to avoid awareness that what is described is *not* there to be described at all. But there are less obvious devices we can pick out from that first chapter. Take this sentence about one of the men trying to read what Tressell calls the *Obscurer*:

> Easton . . proceeded to laboriously work through some carefully cooked statistics relating to Free Trade and Protection, [p. 17 / p.19]

Compare the way those two qualifying phrases are used: 'laboriously' and 'carefully cooked'. You might take 'laboriously' as operating like the opening description, just telling us something that we could all agree on if we were actually there, watching this man: that he is having some difficulty reading the paper. But the other phrase, 'carefully cooked', clearly tells us something over and above a neutral 'description'. This is not something we would know just from looking at the newspaper. We're given an attitude, an opinion, alongside the statement that he is reading statistics. The opinion is the author's or narrator's, and since we, as readers, are not ourselves given any access to those statistics, to judge for ourselves, we're in no position to challenge the claim that they are 'cooked': we just have to take it that they are. But, of course, 'laboriously' is not a neutral description either: it, too, when we think about it, is just as 'carefully cooked' as those alleged statistics.

Another device gives us a less blatantly direct impression of a 'truth'. We're given a description of a number of men, sitting down, in the middle of a working day, to have a cup of tea. We've been told earlier in the chapter that the place where they have their tea is surrounded by jam jars, broken cups, bits and pieces of crockery which are lying around in the dirt of the kitchen, which is also used as the temporary paint-shop. Then we get this sentence:

> Another who took no part in the syndicate was Barrington, a labourer, who, having finished his dinner, placed the cup he brought for his tea back into his

> dinner basket and having closed and placed it on the mantelshelf above, took out an old briar pipe which he slowly filled, and proceeded to smoke in silence,
> [p. 17 / p. 19]

We may not consciously notice the detail as we read, but if we do we are being prompted to ask *why* this man is so singled out, in not using one of the jam jars but a cup, and not a broken or dirty cup but a clean one he has brought with him. Those who have read the novel will know that this detail tells us a lot, retrospectively, about Barrington. But at this point in the novel the detail prompts a question to which we are not given the answer by the voice that is telling us the story. We spot the detail, but are not quite sure what to make of it.

Another device. The men get to talking about the house they are working on, with its odd name, which had after all been in the first sentence of the novel: "The Cave"'. Then this [p.20 / p. 18]:

> "Funny name to call a 'ouse, ain't it? " he said. "'The Cave'. I wonder what made 'em give it a name like that."
> "They calls 'em all sorts of outlandish names nowadays," said old Jack Linden.
> "There's generally some sort of meaning to it, though," observed Payne.

We're not actually told here what the point of calling the house"The Cave" is, but it's made pretty plain that the reader is being invited to think about why *Tressell* called it that.

What I'm trying to illustrate is the various ways in which, in these opening pages, the author, as any author does, uses a variety of devices through which, as we read, we become 'involved' in the story. We begin to learn things, to take them for granted—but we can also be pulled up short and asked to think about them. And we can then be told, or not told, what we are *supposed* to think about them. We can also be given 'exercises', in trying to work out whether what we are being told is the 'truth' or not.

For instance, at one point, Owen, who is to become the spokes-person for one attitude towards socialism, is listening to a conversation among the other men arising out of something in the newspaper. We get this sentence:

> Owen was listening to this pitiable farrago with feelings of contempt and wonder. Were they all hopelessly stupid? Had their intelligence never developed beyond the childhood stage? Or was he mad himself?
> [p. 25 / p. 27]

When we read that phrase, 'this pitiable farrago', are we to take it as what Tressell thinks of the conversation or only of what Owen thinks? Are we being invited to judge whether we agree with Owen here, or are we simply being told that it *was* a pitiable farrago (whether we think so or not)?

The last device I'll briefly comment on comes towards the end of the chapter, when there's an angry exchange in which Owen tries to explain why the people working on the house are in some ways worse off than slaves. He gets this response from one of the older workers:

> "Oh, I don't see that," roughly interrupted old Linden, who had been listening with evident anger and impatience. "You can speak for yourself, but I can tell yer I don't put myself down as a slave."
> "Nor me neither," said Crass sturdily. "Let them call their selves slaves as wants to."

The text goes on:

> At this moment a footstep was heard in the passage leading to the kitchen. Old Misery! or perhaps the Bloke himself! Crass hurriedly pulled out his watch.
> "Jesus Christ!" he gasped. "It's four minutes past one!"
> [pp. 29-30 / p. 31]

Obviously, the author has so arranged the action that it confirms the 'truth' of one of the positions in the argument and undermines the other.

These, then, are among the standard devices of the novelist, deployed by Tressell in those opening pages. There are two basic strategies at work, and they constitute both the strength of the traditional novel and, I think, its dangers. Yet, interestingly, both these strategies are themselves questioned within this very chapter. Notice the earlier argument, about what is meant by 'poverty", in which we get this exchange:

> "Let us begin at the beginning," continued Owen, taking no notice of these interruptions. "First of all, what do you mean by Poverty?"
> "Why, if you've got no money, of course," said Crass impatiently.
> The others laughed disdainfully. It seemed to them such a foolish question.
> "Well, that's true enough as far as it goes," returned Owen, "that is, as things are arranged in the world at present. But money itself is not wealth: it's of no use whatever."
> At this there was another outburst of jeering laughter.
> "Supposing for example that you and Harlow were shipwrecked on a desolate island, and you had saved nothing from the wreck but a bag containing a thousand sovereigns, and he had a tin of biscuits and a bottle of water."
> "Make it beer!" cried Harlow appealingly.
> "Who would be the richer man, you or Harlow?"
> "But then you see we ain't shipwrecked on no dissolute island at all," sneered Crass. "That's the worst of your arguments. You can't never get very far without supposing some bloody ridiclus thing or other. Never mind about supposing things wot ain't true; let's 'ave facts and common sense." [p 28, p 29]

The passage speaks a lot to me because as a student I would get into rows with my Dad about politics or whatever, and say "Look, suppose..." and he'd say: "Forget suppose!" But isn't the novelist essentially *supposing*? Let us suppose there is a house called 'The Cave'; let us suppose there are these men working in it; let us suppose they said this and did this. But when Owen tries that tactic himself within the novel, he's told he can't get anywhere in an argument by reaching for supposes. So how can the novel get anywhere by supposing?

The first basic strategy for the novelist, and basic problem for the reader, is that the novelist can suppose any 'bloody ridiclus thing' he likes (he can make it water or beer, a desolate or a dissolute island, as he wishes), but *we* can't as readers. We're dealing with someone else's made-up fictions and we can't offer some counter-supposition in such a way that it has any effect whatsoever on the rest of the novel. We can exercise our judgement, we can decide for ourselves whether this clean cup or this desire for beer tells us something significant about a character or not—but we don't know whether it makes any difference which way we decide, until we find out somewhere else in the novel that the author thinks it does too.

The second basic strategy is a kind of hierarchy, a setting of levels of authority and 'truth'. The text says something like 'Owen said X', but then we're told that 'Owen really thought Y'. We may then get a further level of comment, from the narrator: 'But what Owen didn't know was Z. ' This is a characteristic pattern in many novels: a hierarchy of truth levels. 'This is true; but this is more true; and this is even more true.' Again, this chapter illustrates, and undermines, that pattern very well at one point:

> "Well, I don't go in for politics much, either, but if what's in this 'ere paper is true, it seems to me as we oughter take some interest in it, when the country is being ruined by foreigners."

Notice that the issue is one of 'truth', and an appeal to what's printed, as an authority. But another voice cuts across:

> "If you're goin' to believe all that's in that bloody rag you'll want some salt," said Harlow.

And then a comment from the narrator:

> *The Obscurer* was a Tory paper and Harlow was a member of the local Liberal club. Harlow's remark roused Crass.

We are clearly to take the description of the paper as itself a true description, but also as affecting the truth of the paper's own claims. The text continues:

> "Wot's the use of talkin' like that?" he said, "you know very well that the country is being ruined by foreigners.... and I say it's about time it was stopped. "
> "'ear, 'ear, " said Linden, who always agreed with Crass, because the latter, being in charge of the job, had it in his power to put in a good—or a bad—word for a man to the boss. "'Ear, 'ear! Now that's wot I call common sense."
> Several other men, for the same reason as Linden, echoed Grass's sentiments... [p. 20 / p. 22]

The pattern is clear here: we are told a statement claiming to be true, but then told the (true) reasons why those who assert it hold it to be true—because it agrees with their politics, or because the man who said it is powerful, or because it looks like 'common sense'. But the basis for the claim in the first instance was what was printed in a newspaper—and that paper, we are told, was 'a Tory paper' and (we have been told earlier) prints 'carefully cooked statistics'. But then the text goes on: 'but Owen laughed contemptuously.' It is, it seems, possible to oppose and even to laugh at these 'truths' of 'common sense' and Tory papers. But on what basis? By relying upon something printed in a different source, a different newspaper? Or in a novel perhaps? But what is the basis for any claims to truth of a novel?

I want to suggest that these basic strategies and various devices are what give us the impression of certain kinds of 'truth' within a novel, but since those devices have been developed within the classical bourgeois novel they raise for me certain problems about any attempt to write a 'working class' novel. At the core of the problem is a relationship between truth and fiction, and even though a novel can indeed put into question its own truth, or its own status as fiction, in the end what the very *form* of a novel seems to resort to is the essential tactic of so arranging a hierarchy of truths within it that some of those truths are confirmed, and some are disconfirmed, by what 'happens' in the novel—but what happens is what the novelist *supposes* to happen. Well, what danger is there in that? And why should it concern socialists anyway? And what's this got to do with a difference between traditional working class politics and what the post-'68 generation detoured into? Let's pursue it a bit further.

Let's suppose we are on a desolate island, says Owen. In one sense that's where (we tend to suppose) the English novel started—with Defoe supposing about a desert island, in *Robinson Crusoe*. So let me sketch, very briefly indeed, some moments in the history of this curious relation between truth and fictions, in the development of the novel. Here's part of what Defoe says in his Preface to *Robinson Crusoe* (1719):

> If ever the story of any private man's adventures in the world were worth making public, and were acceptable when published, the editor of this account thinks this will be so.
>
> The wonders of this man's life exceeds all that (he thinks) is to be found extant; the life of one man being scarce capable of a greater variety.
>
> The story is told with modesty, with seriousness, and with a religious application of events to the uses to which wise men always apply them (viz.) to the instruction of others by this example, and to justify and

> honour the wisdom of Providence in all the variety of our circumstances, let them happen how they will.
>
> The editor believes the thing to be a just history of fact; neither is there any appearance of fiction in it.

Defoe claims that this is a history of fact, that he is only the editor of a true story, one that really happened—and the extraordinary wonders that actually happened reveal, and instruct the reader in, the workings of Providence. Now, clearly, if I want to claim that a story shows the workings of Providence I can't admit that it's a story I simply made up; and conversely, if I admit that the wonders are pure fiction they can hardly be used as evidence for Providence. But Defoe is actually engaged in a double move, both in the assertion of Providence and in a scientific repudiation of the need for miraculous explanations of how the world works, and this complicates the overall relation between truth and fiction.

At one point in the novel Crusoe finds with utter astonishment that corn is growing in his compound, though he hasn't planted any. This must, he thinks, be the action of God, 'the pure production of Providence for my support', and he gives heartfelt thanks to God. But then he remembers something: 'at last it occurred to my thoughts that I had shook a bag of chickens' meal out in that place, and then the wonder began to cease'. He thinks he has found a perfectly rational explanation so stops attributing the corn to Providence. But then, in a further twist, he thinks that perhaps it was indeed Providence which ensured that there should be a few grains at the bottom of the sack, that the divine has been working in 'scientific' ways—and again he thanks God.

It's a classic moment of oscillation between two world-views, two entire explanatory schemas. But what Crusoe's final compromise position excludes, or suppresses, is the awareness that it wasn't God who arranged these events at all: it was Daniel Defoe, who devised the whole incident in the first place and who deliberately offers his readers two alternative explanations of what happened. Yet, fundamentally, Defoe represents himself as not in control at all; as only the editor of a true story.

By the time we get to Henry Fielding's *Tom Jones* (1749), a generation later, Fielding is quite happy to admit that he is offering fiction. Indeed, he cheerfully claims in his opening remarks that since he's inventing this new way of writing, called the novel, he can therefore make up what rules he likes. The reader is entirely under his control, but it's for the reader's own good. Fielding will intervene occasionally, not only to arrange the events of the story, but to tell the reader what really happened, despite any misleading appearances. The reader will gradually become attuned to the rules of the genre and will finally learn to make his or her own judgements in accordance with those rules—and therefore, of course, in basic agreement with Fielding's own judgements, which, necessarily, constitute the 'truth' in the world of this fiction.[4]

Some twenty years later, Horace Walpole—who was incidentally the son of Fielding's great political enemy Robert Walpole—wrote *The Castle of Otranto*, initiating the vogue for the 'Gothic' novel. In the preface to the first edition he claims, like Defoe, to be only editing a manuscript he has found; but he leaves it peculiarly vague whether the manuscript is a true story or a fiction. He claims, with a great deal of circumstantial detail, that it is several hundred years old; but suggests that it was probably written by a priest who wanted to delude people into believing false superstitions; and then concludes: 'I cannot but believe that the groundwork of the story is founded on truth. ' Then, in the preface to the second edition, a few years later, he finally admits that he made up the story—but then claims that since he has observed the correct rules for writing fictions which have the authority of the great writers of the past, he is indeed offering a kind of truth!

A generation or so later, Jane Austen makes fun of the very conventions of the Gothic which Walpole relied upon, and even has an ironic glance at Defoe's notions of

---

4 I have tried to explore some of these aspects of Fielding in my *Reading Relations*, 1982. [Now also in *Legal Fictions*, 2015.]

Providence. In *Persuasion* (1818) we have a blatantly engineered bit of plot coincidence, followed by the comment:

> "Putting all these very extraordinary circumstances together," said Captin Wentworth, "we must consider it to be the arrangement of Providence, that you should not be introduced to your cousin." (ch. 12)

Austen's own title for that novel indicates where the development of the novel has gone. It is concerned with the role and responsibility of persuasion (not scientific proof or religious belief) in society, and it also sets out itself to persuade the reader. It does so primarily by so constructing events and the fates of characters as to show the reader that they should have been persuaded this way rather than that. The final chapter opens:

> Who can be in doubt of what followed? When any two young people take it into their heads to marry, they are pretty sure by perseverance to carry their point, be they ever so poor, or ever so imprudent, or ever so little likely to be necessary to each other's ultimate comfort. This may be bad morality to conclude with, but I believe it to be truth, (ch. 24)

Indeed, yes, we might say. By the end of a Jane Austen novel who can be in doubt about the ending: we know who is bound to marry whom and who is going to be happy and unhappy. But what this claim has to exclude is the fact that in this novel, for example, there was indeed an alternative ending, an ending which Austen wrote and then rejected. And it was, it might seem, open to her to write whatever ending she pleased. The way the novel ends is offered as our basic validation for what we *ought* to believe about these characters. But what we are encouraged to forget is that how the novel ends is already built into what the author *expects* us to believe about those characters. It is not, after all, morality which governs the events, nor truth which decides them, but the author's capacity to persuade us to accept her morality as truth.

It would be possible to track this development further and in more detail.[5] But let me suggest that its apotheosis has been in the dominant forms of film and television. As film took over certain of the functions of the novel in the early part of the twentieth century, what it perfected was a structure of presentation in which we literally 'see' the apparent truth of certain claims made within the film—and what the dominant form of the fiction film goes out of its way to avoid us realising is that the film itself is entirely constructed, that its *effect* of the real is indeed, in a new sense, a matter of editing, the work of an editor. The same case can be made about much television, including the 'non-fiction' of the *News* : we are persuaded of the truth of that news by the apparent match between commentary and visual presentation, as in the nightly bulletins at present on the Dover seamen's struggle, just along the coast from here. But of course what we see on television, what has been edited for us to see, has been selected precisely to endorse what we are being told in the commentary. And we cannot always just go and 'see for ourselves'.

Yet at precisely the point at which film narrative emerges out of the conventions of melodrama and the novel, the novel itself begins to bifurcate, to split into an on-going traditional mode and a break with that dominant form, into what we call modernism. (As it happens, James Joyce, the great exemplar of how the novel finally breaks with the received bourgeois forms, once toyed with the idea of running his own cinema. It's one of several things he shares with his compatriot Robert Tressell/Noonan.) The crucial move in modernist fiction was to insist upon its own fictiveness, to leave the reader in no doubt that he or she was reading a constructed text, to make its devices visible. And at the same time to refuse any simple match between narrative authority, what 'happens', and what judgements the reader is to arrive at about what happens. In that

[5] I have tried to do so in my *Literary Converions* (2015), which reprints part of *The Literary Labyrinth* (1984).

development, the relation between truth and fiction becomes itself part of the play of the fiction, as it had been in, say, Cervantes or Sterne.

Let me close this brief sketch of the novel's history with the two prefatory comments in Alain Robbe-Grillet's *The House of Assignation*:

> The author wishes to make it clear that this novel is in no way intended to be an account of life in the British territory of Hong Kong. Any resemblance, in setting or situation, between the two is a matter of pure coincidence, whether objective or otherwise.

And, on the next page:

> Should any reader, knowing his Far-Eastern ports well, form the opinion that the places described here do not correspond to reality, the author, who has himself spent the greater part of his life there, would advise him to go back and look again: things change quickly in those parts.

It's time to summarise the argument thus far. Given those basic strategies, those various devices, and that fundamental relation between truth and fiction in the dominant form of the novel, there is—I want to suggest—a basic danger involved in the use of the form. Whatever the content of the novel, whatever its ideas, and whatever the reader's attitude to that content, in reading a novel constructed upon such devices we are being attuned, trained, inculcated, at the level precisely of our 'involvement', into accepting two basic procedures.

The first is to 'believe our betters' (to use a phrase from Tressell), that is, to take part in the construction of a hierarchy of truths in which some other person (the author, the narrator) not only is in control of what is happening but also claims to know the truth of what is happening—while we are left, in effect, having to believe what we're told. It's as simple, as basic, and in one sense as harmless, as that. But as the structure of our relation to truth and control, it's far from harmless, and it is arguably that very structure which is constantly and effectively offered to us as the most fundamental model of the society we actually inhabit, not just within the fictional world of the novel but in the world the novel claims to match, to represent. Think of this passage from Tressell:

> From their infancy they had been trained to distrust their own intelligence, and to leave the management of the affairs of the world . . to their betters; and now most of them were absolutely incapable of thinking of any abstract subject whatever. . . Therefore Crass and his mates, although they knew nothing whatever about it themselves, accepted it as an established, incontrovertible fact that the existing state of things is immutable. They believed it because someone else told them so. They would have believed anything: on one condition—namely, that they were told to believe it by their betters. They said it was surely not for the Likes of Them to think that they knew better than those who were more educated and had plenty of time to study.
> [p. 219 / p. 203]

Perhaps it's becoming clearer why working-class students of my generation, who had indeed been given time to study, could feel so suspicious of one of the most familiar and deeply effective modes in which we are indeed told what to believe by our betters.

The second danger is more subtle, and even more implicit. It's not normally very effective at all simply to be told what to believe or what we should do. Tressell recognises this within his own fiction. At one point, for example, Owen runs up the stairs and since he has tuberculosis he's badly out of breath. His small son says, "How many times will Mother have to tell you about it before you take any notice?" [p. 88 / p. 84] But though being told to do something or not to do something tends to be pretty ineffective as a way of actually changing behaviour, being told not to do anything *at all* or, even worse, being told that whatever you do will make no difference, can be decidedly effective. Arguably, the deepest convention of the novel is indeed that we as readers *can* do nothing, that the novel will take its course whatever we think or do, that its working through of its development and *dénouement* is fundamentally 'inevitable'—is, indeed, beyond the control even of its author.

The obverse of inevitability is, of course, passivity, acquiescence, a kind of surrender. A culture which so highly validates the process of merely 'following' a story tends, one might suggest, to produce mere followers. Again, much television can be seen as reinforcing older patterns here. But then simply telling people not to be passive or acquiescent, particularly in a mode which itself endorses passivity at another level, would surely be wholly ineffective. And that problem is endemic to any attempt to write a political novel which activates its readers towards a genuinely democratic mode of socialist politics.[6]

How then does Tressell negotiate these problems? Throughout the novel, he poses precisely the difficulty, which Owen constantly faces, that no matter how many times you *tell* people about socialism, or that socialism is a good thing, or that they ought to become socialists, it has very little effect. But Tressell himself, though he uses—as I've tried to show—the normal devices of the traditional novelist, doesn't simply tell his own readers about socialism; nor does he manipulate the plot to 'demonstrate' the truth of socialism. Instead, he basically offers what I'll call exercises in understanding, which his readers can try out for themselves, within and beyond the text itself.

One obvious such exercise, which is almost an open invitation, is the passage where Hunter, as a fundamentalist preacher, is challenged on his claim that he believes every word of the bible. [p. 249 /p. 231] Faced with the Gospel of

---

6 This is a variant of 'the Mrs. Gaskell syndrome' — a phrase for which I have been gently, and perhaps rightly, chided by Macdonald Daly in his Introduction to the Penguin Classics edition of Mary Barton (1996).

Mark ch. xvi —'if they drink any deadly thing it shall not hurt them'—and a proffered bottle of strychnine, the blustering preacher rapidly backs off. Clearly, the reader is being invited to try the exercise on the next reactionary fundamentalist they come across!

Another obvious exercise is the Great Money Trick (ch. 21), when Owen demonstrates, by using three knives, three half-pennies and some bread, how the working class is exploited by the capitalist class. The reader is clearly being invited to try out the trick on his or her own mates: a trick to be taken out of the pages of the book and performed, rather than simply an argument to be analysed and repeated.

A third exercise is the chapter on the Oblong, where you are in fact given two exercises. The population of the country is divided into loafers, who simply exploit others, those who work but don't produce anything useful, and those who work and do produce useful things. It's an inevitable question, as you read, where you are to classify yourself. (I'm not sure about literary critics.) But that exercise is interrupted by another, and we are given what we take to be Owen's hesitation and doubt:

> He knew they would refuse to try to see the meaning of what he wished to say if it were at all difficult or obscure. How was he to put it to them so that they would *have* to understand it whether they wished to or not? It was almost impossible. . . It would be easy enough to convince them if they would only take a *little* trouble and try to understand... [p. 287 /p. 266]

As a reader, I now have to classify myself as someone who is or isn't prepared to take a little trouble to understand.

The importance of these various exercises is that we are indeed being 'told' things, but in such a way that we have to think for ourselves about them. We are taken into the beginnings at least of a *process* of thought and inquiry, and not just given the result of that process—which is exactly how the Owens teach their own child within the novel. But isn't this just a palliative? Aren't these moments just fragments of essay or treatise inserted into the novel? Isn't

Tressell at these points trying to do what Perry Anderson claimed couldn't be done: to give us adequate concepts in ordinary language? And isn't he trying to do what Jack Mitchell implied shouldn't be done: to use a fictional form merely to get across a message?

At this point, let me back-track to another aspect of both Anderson's argument and the great nineteenth-century novels: the ambition of 'totalisation'. Insofar as the nineteenth-century novels set out to totalise, to give a picture of the entire society, the essential formal problem was to find a focus for that total picture, some central point of intersection which was specific and plausible, and which would act as a believable sampling or representative of the whole, where all the pressures and forces of the society might be seen as converging or revealed. There were various devices for this. One was to centre the novel on a particular character, and favourite candidates for this role in the nineteenth century were, for example, governesses, since they straddled several conflicting positions in the society, as both employee and intimate, as educated yet servant, and as female. The clergyman was another figure in whom several social pressures and determinants could be seen as intersecting. In the early twentieth century the favoured character upon whom to focus the entire novel and the entire society was often the artist figure himself. (To some extent, of course, Tressell's novel is a *Portrait of the Artist as an Artisan*)

Another kind of central focus would be an event: the novel would be structured round some crucial moment, an important historical event like 1848, or something as apparently minimal as a circus coming to town. Another organising focus might be a place, a courtroom, a boardroom, a country house. It's interesting to notice, as Jack Mitchell once pointed out, how often a house has acted as a focus for a novel. I started to pursue this, but realised that my talk at this point might turn into a whole WEA course! Think of *Wuthering Heights*, *Howards End*, *The Big House of Inver*, Shaw's *Heartbreak House*, *Bleak House*, Lettice Cooper's *The New House*, *Brideshead Revisited*, *A Doll's House*,

A House for Mr Biswas, and more recently in America Gaddis's *Carpenter's Gothic* or Tracy Kidder's reportage *House*. The house has been offered as an embodiment of a whole mood and atmosphere, from Gothic mansions to Peake's *Gormenghast*; as a place where people meet to talk, as in W.H. Mallock's *The New Republic*; as a retreat beyond social pressures or as the seething location of them. Think of the ideological role of Lutyens' revival of 'traditional' houses, or of Stately Homes and the Heritage industry today. One can think fairly easily of various familiar ways in which houses have been taken, within novels and in reality, as carriers or foci of meanings and values.[7]

Arguably, Tressell's way of giving his novel its focus was deeply original. The houses in his novel, initially 'The Cave', but then also others, are not just places where the 'action' happens to occur, or where he brings together a variety of characters to have arguments. Nor does he merely use the house as a picaresque device, allowing his characters to move from house to house and thereby through a range of the society, though he does indeed do that. He also uses some of the houses emblematically, so that we see how Sweater's Cave contrasts so markedly in its wealth with the poverty-stricken houses of the men who worked to make the Cave so opulent. We're also brought to see, quite plainly, how the houses themselves are part of the system of exploitation: we're told very explicitly how much old Linden has paid out in rent to Sweater over the years, and how Rushton cheats those who commission the painting and decorating of the houses, by stealing from empty houses, by skimping and over-charging. All this is very plain and emphatic.

But Tressell goes further in two important ways. Since we are also given a direct account of the wage-exchange which controls the work done by the men on these houses, and since the injustice of that wage-exchange is clearly demonstrated by the Great Money Trick, we are led to see very precisely how it is the work done on the houses which

---

7 I have tried to develop some related arguments in *On Joyce* and *On Yeats : Upon A House* (2015.)

generates the surplus for the bosses and the exploitation of the workers: the houses, as work-places, are clearly seen as a site of the fundamental exploitation which is at the centre of the whole social process—and to make the work-process as basic to a novel as it is to society was already to be deeply original.

Moreover, we are not only told this, or given a demonstration of how the analysis applies to the houses in the fiction. The choice of houses, of their building and repairing and decorating, as the basic focus of the novel, ensures that the whole novel acts as a kind of *reflexive exercise* upon the reader—since any reader almost certainly lives in some kind of a house. You cannot read this novel in a house without recognising that its analysis turns upon your own house, upon the very building in which you are reading it. Reading the novel, it's possible to pause and look, literally, at one's own walls for confirmation of its case.

The novel makes you very conscious indeed that a house, any house, is the point where land, land-ownership, land values, finance, investment, interest, inflation, production, employment, labour, law, local government, national policy, individual need, hopes and possibilities, all converge in our daily experience. And that's true whether we rent, own, or squat.

It's true, also, though in a different way, of the building we're in at the moment, assembled here for this Tressell Memorial Lecture. This Queens Hotel, like any building, is not only an emblem of the society we live in: it's also, in itself, a concretisation, an embodiment, of a process of exploitation, of a certain relation between capital and labour. One of the effects of this novel is that once you realise how houses are being used within the novel, you can't go down any street—because any street has some kind of houses in it— without having it brought literally home to you what the nature of capitalism is. I got off the train here an hour or so ago, and in the two minutes it took to walk down Havelock Street I passed seven estate agents, eight solicitors, and the offices of several building societies.

It's now abundantly clear that housing has become, in the 1980s as in the 1880s, one of the crucial intersection points of the politics of our society, whether we think of home-ownership or the sale of council houses, the replacement of rates by a poll tax or the effect of mortgage interests (in both senses) on economic policies. Two fragments: one a report from the *Guardian*, 22 April 1988:

> Mrs Thatcher yesterday told a 73-year old widow who had lost all entitlement to housing benefit because of this month's Social Security changes that she should raise a loan against the security of her unsaleable terraced house in South Wales to help make ends meet. Deprived of housing benefits she is now left with £4 a week to live on. She has been unsuccessfully trying to sell her £15,000 house for 20 months.

Put this alongside a report a few days later (*Guardian*, 25 April 1988):

> The Government has discovered a source of income greater than privatisation, which has always been there, but which no one previously had dared to mine. It is called the poor. A recent paper written for stockbrokers Greenwell Montague states that if the earnings link had been retained married pensioners would now be getting £79.90 instead of £65.90. Greenwell estimates that the saving on State pensions this year will be a startling £4 billion. That £4 billion alone almost matches the income from privatisation proceeds and more than accounts for the £3.6 billion surplus in the Public Sector Borrowing Requirement.

Ragged Trousered Philanthropists indeed! It's one of the extraordinary achievements of Tressell's novel that it should speak so directly to our present political condition—and perhaps an indication of the inadequacy of the political perspectives into which it has been so often assimilated that it should still do so.

In focusing upon the house-building and decorating trade, Tressell resolved some of the major problems of the nineteenth-century novel: he found a focus which was not merely 'representative' of the whole society but genuinely had some immediate application to everyone within the society, and he constructed an organising centre for his novel which derived its persuasive power not from some manipulated plausibility of plot but from its fusion of emblematic suggestiveness and real referentiality. (Both solutions suggest a need for their political counterparts!) At one point within the novel he can say: "Suppose some people were living in a house ——" [p 157 / p 145] and then elaborate an analogy between a badly built house and the present Money System. He can then turn to the actuality of real, not emblematic, houses and argue:

> "In order that these people may live ... it is first of all necessary that they shall have a place to live in... and that's the beginning of the trouble ... "
> [p. 160 / pp. 148-9]

But of course that's only the beginning of the analysis you have to undertake as reader, to think through for yourself.

It's characteristic of that process, that exercise of thinking for yourself that, in the end, no one can think it for you. When I'd arrived at this point in my own argument, I happened to re-read Raymond Williams's foreword to Jack Mitchell's book, written back in 1969. There, I found this typically compressed and laconic comment, which I had read long before but had failed fully to grasp:

> Tressell draws much of his strength from the fact that his workers are a small and therefore immediately visible community and that their relationships to their employers and also to the general social system can be immediately dramatised in the house which they are decorating for somebody else—an unusually visible system of interlocking exploitation and social display.

That 'unusually visible system' is not, in practice, usually quite so visible to us. It's an important literary as well as political achievement of Tressell to make us see the houses all around us as, quite literally, visible evidence for the truth that is brought home to us by his wholly exceptional novel.

*

WRITING BRITAINS

Nineteenth-century British novelists seem, with hindsight, to have had little difficulty choosing a focus of concern, a topic on which to hang their imaginative inquiries into the 'condition of England'. Jane Austen's poised probings of the convergence of classes, finances, and sensibilities through marriage negotiations, George Eliot's provincial cross-sections, Dickens's entrepreneurs and debtors, railways and law cases, Thackeray's social vanities, Trollope's parsonages and cathedral closes, Hardy's determined destinies—all these can appear to have traced the contours of a once shared history, through representative dilemmas, typical figures, emblematic events. The governess and the doubting vicar, the thrusting politician and the autodidact, could come together in a panorama of an apparently common Britain.

But now? What representative focus for imagining being 'British' is now available? Some would claim the obvious primary concern as differentiation and diversity, ethnic and cultural. Contemporary Asian-British novelist Hanif Kureishi emphatically asserts, against George Orwell's complacent 1941 sketch-map of the 'British character', that:

> [Orwell's] tolerant, gentle British whites have no idea ... of the violence, hostility and contempt directed against black people every day by state and individual alike in this land . . it is major adjustments to British society that have to be made. . . I stress that it is the British who have to make these adjustments. It is the British, the white British, who have to learn that being British isn't what it was. (Kureishi 1986: 37-8)

Yet Kureishi himself suggests the too easy notion that only white British have to make such adjustments, side-stepping the problem that the several varieties of non-white British may also have to extend their own notion of 'British' to include a larger complexity.

'Britain's multicultural demography', writes one critic, comprises 'not merely "symbolic ethnicity", the quaint or passing display of cultural wares in "Asian" Leicester, "Bengali" Whitechapel, "Chinese" Liverpool or "Arab" Kensington. A necessary and always deeply threaded, historicity underwrites each' (Lee 1995: 72). A roll-call of 'typical' characters in a contemporary condition of Britain novel might feel constrained to include not only English, Welsh, Irish, Scottish but also Polish, Egyptian, Jewish, Cypriot, Italian, Chinese, Caribbean, Nigerian, Kenyan, Indian, Pakistani, Sri Lankan, Australian, New Zealand, Canadian, American, Maltese, Turkish, Zimbabwean, South African, Falklander . . Nor are ethnic or hybrid identities necessarily the primary focus, given other continuing diversities of class, region, age, gender. A nineteenth-century novelist, returning and surveying, might well regard the received fictional forms as crumbling into unmanageable diversity and complexity.

Mere miscellany, however, offers no form. To justify any social grouping or fictional cast as 'British', however hyphenated, requires some shared framework or apparatus, of overlapping history or common culture. Raymond Williams, a novelist who described himself as a Welsh European, once commented:

> When we hear the word 'culture', some of us reach for our fancy dress. Real life is home, family and a job; wages and prices; politics and crisis. Culture, then, is for high days and holidays: not an ordinary gear but an overdrive. So if you say 'Welsh culture' what do you think of? Of bara brith and the Eisteddfod? Of choirs and Cardiff Arms Park? Of love spoons and englynion? Of the national costume and the rampant red dragon? All these things are here, if at different levels and in different ways. But over and above them is another culture. Not the alien Saxon, who belongs, in truth, with the fancy dress. Not even, in any simple way, the alien or at least different English. Taking culture in its full sense you would be speaking of something quite different: of a way of life determined by the National

> Coal Board, the British Steel Corporation, the Milk Marketing Board, the Co-op and Marks and Spencers, the BBC, the Labour Party, the EEC, NATO. But that's not Welsh culture. Maybe, maybe not. It's how and where most people in Wales are living, and in relation to which most meanings and values are in practice found . . And if we have shared these things with others, that sharpens the question. Where is it now, this Wales? Where is the real identity, the real culture?
>
> (Williams 1989: 99)

Williams was a founding figure in British cultural studies but also wrote several ambitious novels deeply shaped by a political as well as an aesthetic commitment to attempted totalization, to grasping in imagination and analysis a whole social formation. His early work can stand for a form of the novel still in deep continuity with those nineteenth-century procedures and solutions.

The focus of *Border Country* (1960) is the continuing ramifications of an intensely local conflict within the wider 1926 General Strike. *Second Generation* (1964) uses the city of Oxford to embody cultural and political contrasts between middle-class academia and Cowley factory life. In *The Fight for Manod* (1979) the establishment of a new town in Wales focuses not only relations and conflicts within Wales but European-wide economic policies, procedures, and priorities. For though Williams might be claimed as a Welsh novelist, his own emphasis upon a shared 'culture' (in that larger sense) took him conceptually and imaginatively beyond the familiar but problematic boundaries of 'nation'or 'state' and their accompanying assumptions.

His extraordinary final set of novels, *People of the Black Mountains* (1989, 1990), stretches both the received fictional form and our sense of historical continuity and identity. The novel uses a loose framing narrative to layer brief episodic tales upon one minutely mapped area of what is now the border between Wales and England. It is one of the few novels to be read with an Ordinance Survey map to hand: every path, cairn, and ruin within the novel's territory holds a story. This exact local attention organizes an enormous temporal sweep, beginning with neolithic cave communities and moving through several thousand years of imagined histories to break off, with Williams's premature death in 1988, only into the fifteenth century. Unlike the reader, however, the successive generations of inhabitants of this small local terrain are aware of their predecessors only, if at all, as legend, hearsay, distorted folk memories. What is emblematic here is the construction of a shared, inherited, co-existence and several kinds of mutual dependence but with no consciously acknowledged and continuing identity across the dis-continuities, opacities, and partial ignorance. The nation-state is relativized by the sheer sweep of the novel merely to a historically recent, and temporary, construction of identity.

Several related problems lurk as we move to the more recent generation of novelists. The diversity reflected on the shelves of any adequate bookshop questions whether contemporary fictions can appropriately imagine an overarching culture within which such multiple differences operate, or whether the new range simply offers enclosed cultural self-presentations more akin to 'fancy dress' or 'symbolic' ethnicity Moreover, in so far as much of contemporary Britain's multicultural diversity stems from a previous imperial sway, there is also the problem of an asymmetrical relation to an apparently shared history: each ex-colony's relation to that global history was connected to the metropolitan power but not necessarily shared in any specific way with those other histories. This is also an aspect of that question side-stepped by Kureishi: how the several communities within the UK relate not just to the dominant ethos but also to each other. Reading each other's fiction may be part of that wider exploration.

Andrew Cowan's novel *Common Ground* (1996) echoes, not least in its title, Williams's own concerns with the ordinary shape of a whole social experience. Its England would be widely recognizable among a certain class of reader, focused as it is through a year in the lives of a dissatisfied geography teacher and a community arts worker living on the semi-blighted edge of an anonymous town, their mundane miserable-ness shaped by a tight income and a new baby, by rain and waiting for buses, by National Childbirth Trust exercises and reluctant DIY. Cowan's common ground is a sour but not unbearable territory of casual street and playground violence, of vandalized cars and TV-noisy neighbours. The novel offers a downbeat climax in the official violence of bailiffs and police as a campaign to save a local common from a bypass is defeated. Here that nineteenth-century metaphor for devastating change, the railway, has been replaced by the motorway, as the spreading city seeps into a changing countryside, with the transport system itself now as much a lived area as the nineteenth-century parlour. Cowan takes the struggle against the encroaching motorway as the focus for his concerns and characters, most of them deliberately low key and unheroic. The overall tone is self-deprecatingly stoic, a touch away from grim humour. One ironic strand includes a global gesture, as the narrative inter-leaves letters to a brother travelling the world-wide tourist trails, through India, Singapore, Thailand, Guatemala. But neither local nor global strand yields much concluding illumination, transformation, or achievement, only a resisting resignation. This structure of feeling may indeed be familiar and representative of a glum middle England, but it registers only a limited awareness of a terrain outside its specific concerns: the community focused round this common ground contains, for example, few non-white faces.

Timothy Mo's *Sour Sweet* (1982) is a very similar novel of ordinary depressed urban living, in its depiction of an unremarkable family struggling to make a living and bring up the next generation, avoiding all officialdom in the form of even tax returns or driving licences, establishing a bearable living without, it seems, much claim to significance. But Mo's family is immigrant Hong Kong Chinese and the family's life centres on a Chinese take-away, an established feature of the English landscape but still alien territory for most English readers. In that sense the novel opens up an unknown aspect, a glimpse backstage. Sartre once commented on his own temptation as a novelist always to diverge from telling the tale of his central characters to recounting the lives of all those whom they encounter; he instanced the waiter who serves his hero in a restaurant. Mo's Mr Chen begins the novel as an anonymous Soho waiter and is only catapulted into the take-away business by an involuntary debt-entanglement with a Triad gangster gang. The Triad plot allows glimpses into an underworld even less familiar than the kitchen of a Soho restaurant or of a high street take-away, but also operates as exotic fancy dress: Mo's Chinese community can too easily be filtered through reader's lenses borrowed from Kung Fu or James Bond movies, even though Mo deliberately presents the Triads as themselves just another fairly mundane family business, seeking familiar goals of profit maximization, product diversification, and modernization, a banal multinational corporation that happens to be overtly criminal. In this novel it is the non-Chinese who are marginalized, almost all encounters outside that community restricted to the cursory relations of a passing customer. In that respect its horizons are just as restricted as those of Cowan's allegedly common ground.

Hanif Kureishi's film *My Beautiful Launderette* (1985) deploys a parallel device in relation to the Pakistani community in England, again allowing a glimpse behind a familiar high-street facade, this time the Asian-owned launderette. Direct global links come through the central character's extended family relations with Karachi-based wealth and privilege, which emphasizes a business resourcefulness bordering on ruthlessness and an element of sub-criminal dealings which risks highlighting those aspects of the Pakistani community which reinforce white readers' stereotypes. That the relation between the main Asian character and his white lover is homosexual in effect keeps the issue of inter-racial conflict unexpectedly marginal. In Kureishi's novel *The Black Album* (1995) the viewpoint is that of a British Pakistani generation familiar with inter-racial sex and violence, and this novel does overtly overlap cultural communities, as white, black, and Asian groupings occasionally collide and collaborate. However, the dominant cast of Muslim fundamentalist vigilantes and drug-dealing petty gangsters again verges into caricature. The narrative tone of comic confidant hovers between the assurance of a voice articulating a community to those outside it and the anxiousness of someone uncertain of being accepted within it. That the publication of Salman Rushdie's controversial novel *The Satanic Verses* (1988) is used to date the action acknowledges a wider unease at the community's possible reaction to Kureishi's own novel, including its semi-parody of Rushdie's alleged blasphemy when Kureishi's protagonist rewrites the entrusted verses of a guru.

The device of extended family relations deployed by both Mo and Kureishi allows a historical as well as a geographical reach. The autobiographical first novels of second-generation writers often include encounters with, or memories of, an earlier generation's perspective upon a previous homeland and a past imperial history. Some novels may also attempt a direct novelizing of a national history prior to a British re-location. Thus Abdulrazak Gurnah's outstanding *Memory of Departure* (1987) gives vivid glimpses of an East African childhood while his *Paradise* (1994) layers several aspects of East African history into a vividly representative experience. In Fred D'Aguiar's *The Longest Memory* (1994) a complex plantation tale unfolds, with its marvellous interplay of perspectives upon the relation of unknown half-brothers across divisions of skin and the slave/free divide. Ben Okri's *Famished Road* (1991) gives a broad panorama of Nigerian history while A. Sivanandan's *When Memory Dies* (1997) attempts a major novel of Sri Lanka. These variously incorporated histories, precisely through their density and their specificity to one community, highlight the genuine difficulty of combining the global dimension of one community with an adequate awareness of the equally specific but very different cultural inheritances of other communities.

An interesting example is David Dabydeen's *The Intended* (1991), which opens with the overtly encompassing device of a multi-cultural school group:

> It was the regrouping of the Asian diaspora in a South London school-ground. Shaz, of Pakistani parents, was born in Britain, had never travelled to the sub-continent, could barely speak a word of Urdu and had never seen

> the interior of a mosque. Nasim was more authentically Muslim, a believer by upbringing, fluent in his ancestral language and devoted to family. Patel was of Hindu stock, could speak Gudjerati . . . I was an Indian West-Indian Guyanese, the most mixed-up of the lot. There we were together in our school blazers and ties and grey trousers, but the only real hint of our shared Asian-ness was the brownness of our skins. Even that was not uniform. Patel was Aryan, tall, fair-skinned, crisp and cared-for in appearance . . Shaz was stoutly built, shabbily dressed and extremely black; Nasim, slim, was two shades darker than Patel and two shades less immaculate. I, the medium to dark brown West-Indian, was merely clumsy in my schoolclothes.
>
> (Dabydeen 1991: 5)

But though this multicultural group begins almost as a collective protagonist, the narrative 'I' begins to separate out, partly as each character grows into a differentiated adulthood but also, and significantly, as that first-person viewpoint is deepened and particularized by memories of Guyana:

> And truly she was old, her African face sprouting hairs between the cracks, like a golden-apple seed. She was as old as the village, old as the huge tamarind tree, heavy with fruit, that cast a broad shadow over one side of the yard which her father planted when she was a child, and as black as the trench water in which every day of her life she dipped her bucket and took to the house to wash pans, scrub floors, bathe children. Aunte Jessica brought a handful of plums and gave them to me. "Tek some to Englan and when you see white man give him and say you Auntie Clarice send him gift from she back garden in Albion Village, Berbice, Guyana, South America, all the way across the Ocean, you hear, and that he and he race must be kind to you and we, for all body on dis earth is one God's people, not true?". . . She reached into her bosom, searched about, pulled out a handkerchief knotted at one end which she opened to

reveal a five-dollar note creased and humid from being saved up for weeks. She kissed me and put the money in my pocket. As I turned to go she called out a final riddle: "you is we, remember you is we."

(Dabydeen 1991: 39)

None of the others in Dabydeen's carefully differentiated cast is awarded a parallel dimension of memory and cultural specificity. Indeed, the novel acknowledges this thinness in its blatant symbol of inadequate global awareness: Battersea Fun Fair's artificial 'World Tour' where three of the characters converge. Moreover the 'intended' of the title, the white English girl-friend, also remains entirely two-dimensional, without convincing cultural presence of her own, another fantasy of relation. There are no rich memories of England to resonate with those of Guyana.

Part of the difficulty is to know what would count as an appropriate parallel within Britain to these charged and ambivalent memories of overseas imperial dispossession and alternative cultural awareness. The British working class has itself rarely been given that kind of articulation in British fiction, despite several sagas of working-class nostalgia (Catherine Cookson, Roy Hattersley, Katie Anderson). Contemporary working-class experience has found some recent articulation, but within a myopic concentration on such 1990s fashions as football or ecstasy novels.

John King's *The Football Factory* (1996), for example, offers another behind-the-scenes glimpse, this time into the violence-ridden life of football thugs. The novel is shaped around football games, home and away, the central concern of a Chelsea supporters' subculture defined by 'getting pissed, shagging a bird and kicking the fuck out of' other thugs and, where possible, the police, thought of as just another firm of thugs. The dominant mood is utter frustration, endless aggression, mindlessness—yet the text itself is articulately littered with politically correct sentiments and parables. The central strand of repeated match violence alternates with episodic tales incorporating other aspects of footballing culture, including an elderly supporter who punches two young neo-Nazis for abusing a Pakistani family, and an England supporter who ventures beyond away-game travel to find an alternative life in India and Australia. Encounters with black and Asian are predictably violent but the emphasis is not primarily racist, since a black thug is easily accommodated into the Chelsea 'firm'. What remains curious but also symptomatic is the mode of address, combining an assumption of hooligan insiderness with a presumption of impeccably liberal sentiments in the intended reader. Like Kureishi, King seems uneasily to speak for but not to the community he depicts.

King acknowledges a debt to Irvine Welsh's work, most widely known through the film version of *Trainspotting* (1993), which also portrays from within another clearly defined sub-cultural territory in which violence, drugs, and sex are a way of death in life. The primary focus of these novels of housing estates, rave clubs, and street dealing is an age group rather than a regional or ethnic identity. Welsh is one of a wave of new writers, however, who choose to speak both for and to a generation which allows outsiders to eavesdrop only semi-comprehendingly since the accent and vocabulary remain deliberately enclosed. *Disco Biscuits*, edited by Sarah Champion (1997), presents reports from the chemical generation's battlefront, both social and psychological. The prose tends towards streams of syntax-less semi-consciousness from characters who have little perspective outside, or even upon, their own drug-fuelled lives of sex, sweat, noise, daze, movement, within a social environment summed up by, for example, Ben Graham's deliberate clichés:

> This is a skint and dangerous neighbourhood. Flats are regularly broken into or torched; passing cars are pelted with stones; drunken strays at midnight are waylaid with baseball bats and Stanley knives. The pubs are grim, functional alehouses where giros are cashed in return for a few hours of welcome oblivion. Where a desperate middle-aged blues band pound away in the corner, and a hollow-eyed housewife screams vainly at her man to come home while he still has money to put food on the table. Sometimes, clichés are all you have left. Another

> cliché—where there's poverty, fear and desperation, that's where we go to buy our drugs.
>
> (Champion 1997: 164)

This is a last-days mentality, expressed in appropriately hollow poetic prose, and the relation between the restricted horizons of these novels of youth sub-cultures and that of, say, Martin Amis's *The Information* (1995), set in an equally self-regarding and culturally enclosed metropolitan literary world, is depressingly close.

Yet if these are mutually unaware and restricted local cultures what could possibly claim the status of the majority culture? Meera Syal's heroine, the Indian-Derbyshire lass of *Anita and Me* (1996), has no doubt: her ambition of assimilation is defined as being allowed to eat fish and chips and to watch television soaps, both pleasures deeply frowned upon by her respectable immigrant parents. Yet though watching TV does indeed provide the most widely shared cultural framework for most people in Britain, including television adaptations of those sprawling nineteenth-century novels, and television soaps in particular more successfully portray a composite multi-cultural society than most novels, it is rare for a novelist actually to acknowledge that centrality. A comic counter-example is Toby Litt's *Adventures in Capitalism* (1996), which features characters who, for example, attempt to believe and obey all television adverts or who write letters to the characters in those adverts. Litt's Britain is one where all social experience is filtered through publicity images, consumerist enticements, and advertising jingles. His fiction remains, correspondingly, fragmentary.

Julian Barnes's *England, England* (1998) takes the more ambitious step of imagining an England wholly transformed into such a media-shaped construction. Its central plot concerns a megalo-maniacal billionaire who buys up or replicates every well-known tourist attraction and relocates it to the Isle of Wight, now a commercially owned statelet and renamed 'England, England'. In a parodic variation on Williams's territorial device in *Black Mountains*, Barnes situates Stonehenge, Windsor Castle, Manchester United football club, the Houses of Parliament, Buckingham Palace (including its re-deployed royals) all within walking distance of each other, so that tourists need no longer endure the actuality of travel in the real England to sample Devon teas, London taxis, Cotswold cottages, and the Changing of the Guard, within the compass of a single theme park. The satire turns partly upon the reader's uneasy sense that England has already been so transformed, but Barnes's own counter-vision of a post-industrial Britain offering a regressive Utopia is wholly uncompelling. It may well be that any contemporary attempt to capture and focus the 'condition of England' in such a traditional fictional form can itself only offer a form of cultural nostalgia and tourism

Geoff Ryman's extraordinary *253* (1998) was, however, originally published as a hyper-fiction on the Internet, which allowed the possibility of deploying devices reminiscent of both Williams's strategy and Sartre's dilemma. Here a London tube-train provides the physically shared terrain, complete with maps and diagrams. Seven tube carriages carry a total of 253 passengers, each of whom is given one page of 253 words, comprising a brief description of their outward appearance (as they might be seen by other passengers), some biographical information, and an inward account of what each is currently wishing, dreaming, hoping, planning. This overall device allows a plausibly wide roll-call of identities and backgrounds, preoccupations and destinies, to be literally juxtaposed while the hyper-text links allow the reader-browser to explore multiple inter-woven connections not apparent even to the travellers themselves: some passengers are related, about to meet, once knew each other, work for the same firm, are travelling to the same exhibition, will take each other's places, etc. The usual small incidents of commuter travel create momentary trivial encounters and interactions while, as readers, we gradually realize that these lives are also shaped by larger forces beyond the perception of each—including the fact that this train will soon crash. Ryman's work successfully, and humorously, captures the real diversity of urban Britain with its oddly optimistic mode of contemporary co-existence, a combination of mild curiosity about and deliberate semi-ignorance of others, a structure of feeling precisely shaped and regularly reinforced by commuter travel. It is encouragingly characteristic of that sensibility that we reassure ourselves that most of *253*'s passengers will get off before the crash actually comes, to survive and continue their apparently independent but repeatedly interconnected lives.

From Raymond Williams to Geoff Ryman there may be a certain continuity of theme: a recognition of people as living within a shared physical location under common constraints yet with little conscious or deliberate connection, a common ground but little actually held in common. Yet neither total indifference nor only intolerance holds sway, merely a daily contact, an inherited co-existence. Like the planet itself, on this perspective, the nation-state seems more a condition of mutual dependence than any common culture. It is then hardly surprising that contemporary novelists' various attempts at imagining a Britain or writing the experience of some fragment of it may not share any overarching cultural frame or even a common audience, but merely a publishing apparatus, also in decline. Before we attach too much significance to the efforts of novel writers, we should perhaps remind ourselves that, after all, before the award of the 1998 Booker Prize the eventual winner had sold barely a thousand copies, and that was more than the rest of the short-list put together.

REFERENCES :

Amis, Martin (1995), *The Information*
Atkinson, Kate (1995), *Behind the Scenes at the Museum*
Barnes, Julian (1998), *England, England*
Champion, Sarah (ed.) (1997), *Disco Biscuits*
Cowan, Andrew (1996), *Common Ground*
Dabydeen, David (1991), *The Intended*
D'Aguiar, Fred (1994), *The Longest Memory*
Gurnah, Abdulrazak (1987), *Memory of Departure*
—— (1994), *Paradise*
Hattersley, Roy (1990), *The Maker's Mark*
King, John (1996), *The Football Factory*
Kureishi, Hanif (1995), *The Black Album*
—— (1986), *My Beautiful Launderette*
Litt, Toby (1996), *Adventures in Capitalism*
Mo, Timothy (1982), *Sour Sweet*
Okri, Ben (1991), *The Famished Road*
Rushdie, Salman (1988), *The Satanic Verses*
Ryman, Geoff(1998), *253 : the print remix.*
—— http://www.ryman-novel.com.
Sivanandan, A. (1997), *When Memory Dies*
Syal, Meera (1996), *Anita and Me*
Welsh, Irvine (1993), *Trainspotting*
Williams, Raymond (1960), *Border Country*
—— (1964), *Second Generation*
—— (1979), *The Fight for Manod*
—— (1989), *People of the Black Mountains, i: The Beginning*
—— (1990), *People of the Black Mountains, ii: The Eggs of the Eagle*
—— (1989), 'Welsh Culture", BBC Radio 3,27 Sept.1975, published in Williams, *Resources of Hope*

*

INSIDE THE IMPASSE

Raymond Williams & NLR, *Politics and Letters*, New Left Books, 1979.

> The reason for the intense significance that Ibsen possessed for me then was that he was the author who spoke nearest to my sense of my own condition at the time. Hence the particular emphasis I gave to the motif of coming 'to a tight place where you stick fast. There is no going forward or backward.' That was exactly my sensation. The theme of my analysis of Ibsen is that although everybody is defeated in his work, the defeat never cancels the validity of the impulse that moved him; yet that the defeat has occurred is also crucial, (p.62)[1]

The speaker is Raymond Williams, looking back in 1977 on his preoccupations as a Cambridge undergraduate facing Finals exams in 1946, then aged 25, an ex-tank commander completing an English degree interrupted by four years of war service.

> The Manifesto was just testing the water. What has to be introduced into the socialist vocabulary is the notion of defeat.[2]

Again Raymond Williams, in 1973, looking back on his collaborative editing of the May Day Manifesto of 1967-68 and arguing that it hadn't 'failed' — it had been defeated.

---

[1] The interviewers were Perry Anderson, Anthony Barnett, and Francis Mulhem, here referred to collectively as NLR. Page references are to this volume un;less otherwise stated.

[2] Interview with Williams in *Times Higher Education Supplement*, 4 May, 1973, p. 8.

> Hardy is remarkably contemporary with Ibsen in his presentation of a wholly valid and never questionable desire, which is quite tragically defeated without cancelling the validity of that impulse, and which reaches the point of questioning the social order that has defeated it. (p.222)

Again, the theme of defeat, joining literature, desire and social order in a difficult dialectic and suggesting a deep pattern linking Williams's work in drama and the novel: Ibsen as disturbing starting-point in *Drama from Ibsen to Eliot* (1952, rev. 1968), Hardy as crucial hinge in *The English Novel from Dickens to Lawrence* (1971).

In these books it is the breaking and straining of dramatic and fictional conventions, the effort to bend and modify a received form, that focuses the critical treatment and from which Williams, as himself novelist and dramatist, seems to want, stubbornly, to learn. The difficulties of explaining or advancing such formal transformations remain desperately opaque, driving Williams himself to a probing, oblique, wary account:

> ... I think the relation between signification and referent in one's own situation differs from that in any other... in the whole process of consciousness — here I would put a lot of stress on phenomena for which there is no easy knowing because there is too easy a name, the too easy name is 'the unconscious' — all sorts of occurrences cut across the established or offered relations between a signification and a reference. The formalist position that there is no signified without a signifier amounts to saying that it is only in articulation that we live at all. Now maybe this is just a generalization from my own history, but I have found that areas which I would call structures of feeling as often as not initially form as a certain kind of disturbance or unease, a particular type of tension, for which when you stand back or recall them you can sometimes find a referent. . . For all that is not fully articulated, all that comes through as disturbance, tension, blockage, emotional trouble seems

> to me precisely a source of major changes in the relation between the signifier and the signified, whether in literary language or conventions, (p. 167-8)

Stand back a moment from this tangle of direct quotations. Think of Williams's work, across the span of his twenty books. The novels struggle with a received and largely endorsed form (call it loosely, for now, realism), but many of the others radically recast or audaciously invent their formal character.

Long Revolution deploys an unprecedented structure. *Modern Tragedy* immodestly includes a modern tragedy. *Keywords* practically re-defines the notion of dictionary. *Drama in Performance* proposes and performs a then-new procedure of historical analysis. *Culture and Society* defies library labelling. The range of Williams's work — conventionally classifiable as 'political intervention, cultural theory, history of ideas, sociology, literary criticism, analysis of drama, semantic inquiry, novels, plays and documentary film scripts' (NLR Foreword) — has necessitated this formal inventiveness, if only because this 'range' is rarely dispersed, with disparate elements allocated to different writings; instead, each work interweaves, layers, juxtaposes, enacts. This trans-disciplinary ambition provided the title of Williams's 1947 periodical *Politics and Letters* and NLR now revive that title for a book that is itself an innovation in the formal conventions of publishing: a 400-page interview with a single author.

But that form itself needs probing, its possible politics require unpacking. A central procedure of the book is to confront Williams with an extract from his own writings and then to grill him, in detail. An air of inquisition is often coupled here with a whiff of old examination papers: the trap quotation followed by 'Justify or refute'. But Williams is a very old hand at this kind of exercise: he discriminates, qualifies, parries, or concedes, and his final grade is never really in doubt, a clear Upper Second at least. He has, after all, been a teacher since 1946. Perhaps NLR should have been more alert to that other preoccupation of the undergraduate Williams:

> I did a comparison of Eliot and Lawrence in the paper ... I take two passages from Eliot and two passages from Lawrence and . . argue that you cannot deduce the quality of a writer from the analysis of a selected passage since . . if you run one pair, George Eliot appears a better writer, and if you run the other pair, Lawrence emerges as the better writer, (p.62)

By pinning Williams down to quotable passages and formulations the NLR interviewers almost preclude themselves from entering that area of unease, disturbance, blockage, emotional trouble, that seems to have generated Williams's constant engagement with form and with 'politics'.

More substantially, the device of continually questioning Williams and the decision to focus so fully upon his past work allows the NLR voices to evade, in quite noticeable ways, many of the trickier issues they raise. Either Williams's response is left hanging as they move to another question, another quotation (e.g. p. 93 on the Communist Party in the 1950s, p. 366 on the editorial take-over of *NLR* itself, p. 412 on 'class struggle' and 'class conflict'), or the interviewers respond not at the political level posed back to them by Williams but rather by a correction of his examples or formulations (e.g. pp.403f. where Williams pushes a question about the Chinese Cultural Revolution through to the crucial issue of manual and mental labour, only to be fended off by an NLR analysis of the Cultural Revolution itself).

At times Williams's own classification of the 'three marxisms' recently at work in Britain seems worryingly apposite: he offers his interviewers the possibility of an exchange in terms of 'operative theory' (theoretical analysis of the specificities of British late capitalist society, of the consequent situations and agencies of socialist practice...) but his interlocutors pursue instead the lines of 'legitimating theory' (seeking to discover 'the legitimate inheritance of an authentic marxism') or even of 'academic theory' (their recurrent concern with Trotsky seems itself tinged with such academic or legitimating priorities). Of course, the interviewers can also, and impressively, engage with and challenge Williams directly and appropriately. The reply on 'signification' stimulates a two-page response that brings together Sartre on Flaubert, Althusser on ideology, the notion of hegemony, and an analysis of the crisis of the 1840s—which Williams then counters with a compressed history of the political use of statistics. Another exchange begins from Marx's phrase "rural idiocy" and travels via various 19th century counter-revolutionary peasant mobilisations to derelict factories in contemporary Italy (pp. 318-22). Bearing in mind again, therefore, Williams's subversion of quotations, one can readily acknowledge that *Politics and Letters* can seem, at the local level of the actual reading response, both excitingly fertile and remarkably muffled and evasive. Yet still the enterprise as a whole seems, somehow, to go awry.

So let us step further back, and consider the overall shape, the formal structure of the book. It is divided into five sections: Biography; Culture (3 books); Drama (2 books); Literature (4 books plus novels); Politics. As a way of tackling an *oeuvre* so deeply interdisciplinary that's a fairly inert arrangement—and indeed most connections between sections go unremarked or arise only casually, in the interstices of other issues. There seems, in fact, no pressure of political engagement, no real standpoint or position, which motivates this patly predictable organisation.

Its limits can be illustrated by what gets squeezed to the margins, even in terms of texts. Williams's *Television: technology and cultural form* gets one index entry, directing us to a discussion of television drama. Yet television, as a dominant site of the production of ideology, raises intricate questions of an 'operative' kind (the specificities of late capitalism, the situations and agencies of socialist practice) and also invites a detailed re-articulation of classical problems in marxist methodology (the base/superstructure issue at its most entwined) — yet in *Politics and Letters* television is edged merely into 'drama', is barely present under 'Politics', isn't probed as a crucial, culminating nexus of Williams's whole work on 'culture'.

Correspondingly, Williams's most ambitious and direct political intervention, the *May Day Manifesto,* merits only two short discussions, one confined to brief questions and largely anecdotal replies, the second revolving round specific passages in *MDM* on Parliament, on bureaucracy, on 'evolution versus revolution'. The issues raised in both discussions are formidable and fundamental in their ramifications — yet the interviewers seem mainly content to register the textual inadequacies and to recognise the organisational 'failure' while avoiding any explicit consideration of the nature and extent of the 'defeat' of the whole *Manifesto* enterprise—a defeat arguably inscribed in the whole trajectory of Williams's basic project: the option for 'politics and letters', the role of the intellectual today, whose "interventions' take place primarily on the writing table, even when what is written is a Manifesto. (A detailed comparison with the conditions and career of a rather earlier *Manifesto* might have provoked a more cogent analysis and questioning of Williams's whole work.)

What, then, does this overall shape and this tactic of interviewing answer to? It seems designed, or adopted, to avoid a substantial interchange, an exploration and testing of the present positions of both sides. By this asymmetrical and retrospective inquisition NLR can keep their own political cards so close to their collective chest that they all but disappear inside their rib-cages, while Williams can elaborate and elucidate his past positions without ever having to engage fully with a definite alternative position offered by his interviewers: they feed him fragments only. So why did NLR initiate the project in the first place?

The Foreword's claim that 'the present volume is a natural and necessary extension' of the task pursued by *NLR* over fifteen years — 'a systematic enterprise of introduction and evaluation of the main schools within continental marxism' — rings slightly hollow, as if 'turning to consider the pre-eminent intellectual representative of socialism in contemporary Britain' (p.9) were merely the long-planned completion of some pantheon roll-call (Althusser, Benjamin, Colletti, Debray till, finally, Williams, X, Y, Z).

Isn't it rather that those fifteen fertile years have returned us almost full circle, that the sharp surgery of Anderson himself has recently left 'Western Marxism' on its death-bed while Althusserianism quickly fades into memory as a bad case of intellectual measles, an adolescent *rite de passage* that leaves largely unchanged the persistent, pressing, and somewhat bleak, problem: what do we do next? (The posters today proclaim an Anti-Nuclear Week, CND has acquired a new prefix, the *Guardian* correspondence columns have a nostalgic tinge — it isn't quite 1957, but . .) In the impasse that has overshadowed them for so long, NLR have indeed turned to 'the pre-eminent intellectual representative' of a certain tradition of socialist thinking in Britain—only to find, perhaps, a more profoundly considered impasse than their own.

When NLR dissect a *Manifesto* formulation about 'the government, civil service, judiciary, finance and business' they point to one glaring absence from this list: the officer corps, and ask, a shade primly, 'What explains this silence on the central coercive machinery of capital? ' (p. 416). A few pages later the ex-captain in the Guards Armoured Division comments:

> I know what a modem army can do from my own experience: even in the most brutal acts of civil repression that we have seen in Britain, the army has been fighting with one finger and not both hands. Even in Vietnam certain ultimate weapons were held back. On the other hand, I also know, with the advantage of having fought in tanks going into a city, that once an army is dispersed against an enemy that is not concentrated in a single target, it is nothing like as formidable. (p. 422).

Earlier, remembering his own quasi-professional response to the deployment of tanks in Czechoslovakia, Williams remarks 'The left has thought very little about the range of situations in which the nature of force and the use of violence are actually defined' (p.90). Parts of this book at least suggest that necessary process of thought—and without it the analyses of the 'repressive state apparatus' can multiply, perhaps till doomsday, to little avail. That is one facet, one index of a lurking impasse.

'Always there was the image of the tank', says Williams, thinking back to his own war experiences and to British tanks in Greece in 1944, Russian tanks in Berlin in 1953, in Prague in 1968. The image of the armoured car is prominent in Williams's latest novel *The Volunteers*, set in 1987, and this time the streets concerned are British (actually Welsh, a point requiring a whole essay to itself). In Williams's realist fiction the tones have always been slightly dark; now they are deepening further, but in trying to think just beyond the edge of the present, Williams is at least facing correctly, if necessarily in imagination, as fiction, an area the Left tends to leave in a fog of imprecise expectations. Williams's probing of the possibility, in Britain, of a wide extension of mere 'militant particularism' combined with a firmly ensaddled repressive regime (fortified with sophisticated media manipulation) may not be encouraging, but his novel's possible future does not seem only a reflex occurrence of the theme of defeat. It indicates another facet of a looming impasse.

The impasse anticipated novelistically in *The Volunteers* drives us further back however; for why has a militant socialist so consistently adopted the novel as carrier of some of his most sustained political analyses? Why this basic option for 'letters' as a mode of 'politics'? In 1945 Williams had the chance of a parliamentary seat (p. 33). He turned it down; his option then (and still) was to write novels, to edit *Politics and Letters*, to teach. Twenty years later, the Williams whom the *Sunday Times* had depicted, in a front page story, as a major ideological mentor of the new 1964 Labour government not only found himself utterly ignored by that administration but was reduced to angrily and absolutely impotently lobbying a left-wing Labour MP about the government's Vietnam policy (pp.371-2 : his final break with the Labour Party came in 1966). Fully to explore both that option and that impotence (and, of course, their interconnection) would perhaps have brought both NLR and Williams rather harshly up against the fundamental impasse of the 'socialist intellectual' in this society: precisely that deep divorce within the socialist movements between 'mental and manual labour'' which Williams raises in relation to China. That is not a 'failure' but a persistent defeat.

Which brings us back to Ibsen and to Hardy. Why should the Williams of 1945, and since, so constantly pull back to that structure of feeling he locates in Ibsen and Hardy? It would be interesting to attempt an analysis in terms drawn from another figure with whom Williams has acknowledged an affinity. In Lucien Goldmann's work the emergence of a 'tragic vision' in both Pascal and Kant is related in each case to the ambivalent position of a displaced fraction of a class that was, in a larger perspective, on the brink of actually consolidating its power: first the court-lackeys of 17th century absolutism, and then the commercial bourgeoisie of industrial capitalism. One might be tempted to extrapolate this argument to today. Since the 1880s, the European working class has been at least poised for power, against a class still in control enough to 'defeat' but not to vanquish it; while that unstable stalemate persists a 'tragic vision' is likely to emerge, repeatedly, in that displaced fraction of intellectuals who pit themselves, in writing, against the dominant bourgeois order. Even Gramsci is most readily remembered in that formula for a tragic vision: pessimism of the intellect, optimism of the will..

For various reasons, however, I think such an analysis would be misguided; it is offered here merely to highlight the most basic and disturbing inadequacy of this volume. For even a sketchy Goldmannian analysis of the position of Williams would at least propose a theoretically-informed methodological framework within which the overall historical conjuncture could be brought to bear upon the specific significance of a writer. By contrast, and despite fifteen years of intellectual paradigm-shifts and successive theoretical allegiances, NLR seem to have no coherent methodological approach which could inform—structure, give shape to—these interviews with Williams. They therefore are unable really to get beyond the piece-meal limitations of the interview procedure (and even deploy some depressingly familiar biographical crescendo devices) in order to explore the fundamental character of that strategic commitment encapsulated in the weak link of their title: politics *and* letters. Beyond the details of the inquisition, the overall strategic force of that 'and' remains uncertain and opaque, while the relation between Williams's bending of the received forms of socialist discourse and the persistent 'impulse' that has dogged him remains unclarified.

These blocks, limitations, silences, in the book do not invalidate the 'impulse' behind it, nor do they proscribe the eventual potential of the form. But I hope that any sequel will not be more interviews with an X, a Y, or a Z but rather an equally lengthy discussion that begins where this volume ends: on 'the two roads to change'.[3] A published argument about strategy and tactics between, say, Williams, Thompson, Hobsbawm, Anderson, Nairn, (and, maybe—an acid testing of the impasse?—half-a-dozen militants not primarily engaged in 'mental labour') could be a valuable contribution from New Left Books to that 'operative theory' that Williams has struggled towards with such impressive tenacity. *Politics and Letters* could then be seen, like its predecessor, as, very usefully but very preliminarily, 'just testing the water'.

*

[3] Cf. R. Williams, 'Notes on British Marxism since the War', *New Left Review* 100, Nov.1976-Jan.1977. In this article Williams responds indirectly to criticisms of 'populism', 'culturalism' and 'reformism' in his work. Cf. *Politics and Letters*, p.363 for a somewhat ironical comment on Williams's original hopes, at the founding meeting, for what *New Left Review* might have achieved by its hundredth issue.